FLIP-iT-OVER
GUIDES TO TEEN EMOTIONS

A Guys' Guide to

Love

John Logan

Enslow Publishers, Inc.
40 Industrial Road
Box 398
Berkeley Heights, NJ 07922
USA

http://www.enslow.com

Library of Congress Cataloging-in-Publication Data

Logan, John.
  A guys' guide to love / John Logan. A girls' guide to love / Dorothy
Kavanaugh.
      p. cm. — (Flip-it-over guides to teen emotions)
  No collective t.p.; titles transcribed from individual title pages.
  A guys' guide to love and A girls' guide to love will be published
together in a reversible-book format.
  Includes bibliographical references and index.
  ISBN-13: 978-0-7660-2855-5 (alk. paper)
  ISBN-10: 0-7660-2855-0 (alk. paper)
  1. Interpersonal relations in adolescence—Juvenile literature. 2.
Emotions in adolescence. 3. Teenage boys—Psychology—Juvenile
literature. 4. Teenage girls—Psychology—Juvenile literature. 5.
Love—Juvenile literature. I. Kavanaugh, Dorothy, 1969- Girls' guide to
love. II. Title. III. Title: Girls' guide to love.
  BF724.3.I58L64 2008
  155.42'4241—dc22
                               2008007665

Printed in the United States of America.

10 9 8 7 6 5 4 3 2 1

Produced by OTTN Publishing, Stockton, N.J.

To Our Readers: We have done our best to make sure all Internet Addresses in this book were active and appropriate when we went to press. However, the author and the publisher have no control over and assume no liability for the material available on those Internet sites or on other Web sites they may link to. Any comments or suggestions can be sent by e-mail to comments@enslow.com or to the address on the title page.

Enslow Publishers, Inc., is committed to printing our books on recycled paper. The paper in every book contains 10% to 30% post-consumer waste (PCW). The cover board on the outside of each book contains 100% PCW. Our goal is to do our part to help young people and the environment too!

Photo Credits: © iStockphoto.com/Joshua Blake, 6; © iStockphoto.com/Justin Horrocks, 32; © iStockphoto.com/Oktay Ortakciogiu, 4; © iStockphoto.com/Oleg Prikhodko, 20; © 2008 Jupiterimages Corporation, 12, 15, 19, 23, 30, 38, 39, 49; © Photodisc/Getty Images, 41, 57; Used under license from Shutterstock, Inc., 1, 3, 9, 10, 21, 25, 28, 31, 33, 34, 42, 44, 45, 50, 52, 54.

Cover Photo: Used under license from Shutterstock, Inc.

CONTENTS

CHAPTER ONE

This Thing Called Love

> *Greg and Kaela have lived next door to each other since he moved into the neighborhood, when he was five years old. They had been good friends forever, it seems. But one day a few weeks ago, Greg realized that Kaela meant much more to him than just a friend. All of a sudden, he realized that he wanted to spend more time with her and see her more often. He had always known that there was a special bond between them, but this was something different. He had never felt this way about anyone before.*

Among the most important aspects of your life are your relationships with others. Friendship is a relationship in which you can feel relaxed and comfortable. But sometimes a friendship becomes something more. It can be confusing, exciting, frustrating, and complicated. All these feelings can be an important part of love.

Greg started to feel something more for Kaela.

You and Your Emotions

A part of everyone's personality, emotions are a powerful driving force in life. They are hard to define and understand. But what is known is that emotions—which include anger, fear, love, joy, jealousy, and hate—are a normal part of the human system. They are responses to situations and events that trigger bodily changes, motivating you to take some kind of action.

Some studies show that the brain relies more on emotions than on intellect in learning and in making decisions. Being able to identify and understand the emotions in yourself and in others can help you in your relationships with family, friends, and others throughout your life.

Like Greg, you may be finding yourself attracted to a girl whom you have known for a long time. But for reasons that you can't explain, you now feel there is something different about her. All of a sudden, you want to learn all kinds of things about her that you didn't care about before, such as her favorite color, TV shows, and movies. You're curious about what she likes to do in her spare time, what she does with her friends, and just about anything else about her.

Along with these desires of wanting to know her better come fears. You may be afraid of her reaction if she finds out that you feel this way. It can be really embarrassing if she doesn't feel the same way or if she rejects you. Or maybe you're scared that she does feel the same way—and you don't want to mess things up by saying the wrong thing.

When you're feeling attracted to someone, you can undergo an overload of powerful emotions. And that can be hard to deal with. But try to relax. Keep in mind that your peers—your friends and classmates—are going through the same thing. In fact, most people you know—even your parents—have had similar experiences. They've survived and you will, too!

Understanding yourself. Just take a deep breath, and think about what's going on right now in your life. Things are probably pretty stressful. After all, all kinds of changes are happening to you right now—both in your body and in your mind. You're about to deal with or may already be dealing with puberty—the stage of life when your body matures and changes into that of an adult.

In boys, puberty occurs between the ages of ten and fifteen. It is a time of rapid growth and physical change. You and other guys grow taller, get heavier, and develop more muscles. Your voice gets deeper, and hair starts sprouting on your chin. These changes take place at different rates for different guys. But it is common for guys to be feeling uncomfortable at times as certain body parts are growing and changing shape.

The rapid growth that occurs during puberty is due to increasing amounts of hormones in your body. Hormones are chemical substances that carry messages regulating the activity of cells. In boys, increased amounts of the

Puberty can be a confusing and stressful time. Remember, everyone else is going through it, too.

The Chemicals of Love

While love is most commonly associated with the heart, most of the real action is in the brain. Studies have shown that when a person has strong feelings towards someone else, the brain releases increased amounts of certain chemicals called neurotransmitters. One of these neurotransmitters is dopamine. High levels of dopamine are associated with feelings of interest and excitement.

Being exposed to exciting new things can also trigger the release of dopamine in the brain. So if you take your date on some wild rides at the amusement park, it's likely you'll have a second date with that person. The dopamine released during an exhilarating rollercoaster ride, for example, can also stimulate feelings of attraction.[1]

hormone testosterone cause changes and growth that are part of becoming a man.

But these changing hormone levels don't affect just your body. They also affect your emotions. As the amounts of hormones in your body change, you can feel emotional upheavals and experience extreme mood swings. At times you may be feeling really moody and irritable. But at other times you may feel excited and thrilled, like you're on top of the world. That kind of feeling often happens when you feel strongly attracted

Puberty is the developmental stage of life during which the human body is maturing to adulthood. In boys, puberty generally starts between the ages of ten and fifteen.

According to the ancient Greeks, there are three kinds of love:

Phileo—A casual type of love between friends.
Agape—A deeper, unconditional type of love.
Eros—Sexual love.

to someone else. These feelings can be physical, affecting sexual behavior and desire. They can also be emotional, involving a longing for closeness and feeling connected to someone else.

Understanding love. So what exactly are these romantic feelings? What is this thing called love? Trying to understand love can be challenging, but by taking some time to think about what love means to you, you will better understand what is important to you and to the people in your life. You'll also have a better idea about how to keep your relationships strong.

Simply put, love is hard to define. If you asked people in the street what love is, you would probably not get the same answer from any two people. One generally accepted definition is a strong affection for another arising out of kinship or personal ties. That definition basically covers the love you feel for family members and for your friends.

Love of family and friends. A big part of your life is the bond you have with your parents, your brothers and sisters, and friends. The love that you have for and receive from your family members and friends revolves around caring and support. In families with good relationships, this means parents, brothers, and sisters provide emotional support for each other. They take the time to sit down and listen to each other's problems, and try to help work out solutions.

A similar kind of support can also come from friends. As you've grown older, you may have noticed that a special bond has developed among you and your best friends. You enjoy spending a lot of time with them. You all may share secrets or jokes that bring you even closer together. And you probably count on your friends being there for you during rough times, just as you will be there for them.

Romantic love. Although the basic elements of caring and support remain the same, the love you feel for family and friends is very different from romantic love. The person you love is someone you believe you can rely on, who will

If you maintain a good relationship with your father, you will benefit from his love and support.

This Thing Called Love

support and be there for you when you need him or her. But in romantic love there is also a physical attraction and an emotional connection. It is a special bond. When song composers, writers, and filmmakers create songs and stories about love, they are usually referring to this intense attraction and romantic relationship between two people.

How and why romantic love develops between any two people is not known. Someone may say he has never felt "in love" even after dating the same person for several months or even years. Another couple may claim they fell in love the first moment they saw each other. And, once established, every loving relationship is different. The two people involved are individuals who bring their own values and expectations to the relationship.

When romantic love enters your life, it can be an exciting and intense time. That initial feeling of attraction can make you feel like you're on top of the world.

Getting to know someone else through a loving relationship can be an exciting and intense time. Depending upon what's going on in the relationship, your feelings when in love can range from the high exhilaration of knowing someone really loves you to the depths of despair during a breakup. You have the opportunity to learn a lot about yourself while developing and sustaining a new relationship, as you make decisions while in the midst of managing powerful emotions. The way you relate to someone close to you can help your relationship change and grow, or it can end it.

Being attracted to someone is the first step on your journey towards discovering what love is all about. Your experiences in a loving relationship will shape you into the kind of person you will become in the future.

CHAPTER TWO

A Big Crush

Josh is having trouble concentrating in his classes—at least the ones that Lauren is in. In the lunchroom he tries to get a seat close enough to Lauren so that he can try to say a few words and make her notice him. But she's one of the most popular girls in school, and Josh doesn't fit in with her group of friends. Still, he knows he really likes Lauren. What can he do?

What Josh is feeling is a crush—an intense feeling of attraction to another person. He doesn't even know Lauren, but he has these strong feelings for her. He'd really like to get to know her better.

Having a crush on someone who may not even know you're alive can be a real challenge.

Almost everyone, at one time or another, has had a crush. It may simply be an infatuation—an intense, but brief admiration for another person. A crush may not ever lead into anything, particularly if you keep your feelings to yourself. But sometimes a crush can be the beginning of an exciting new relationship.

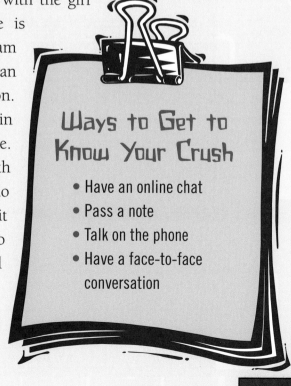

"That's why they call them crushes. If they were easy, they'd call them something else."

—from the 1984 film *Sixteen Candles*

Crushes usually just happen. Suddenly you realize that you really like the way she smiles, or the direct way she stares into your eyes. You find yourself daydreaming about your crush, imagining what you would say during a conversation with her in the hallway at school. Or you might think about being on a date together.

But if you spend no time with the girl you have a crush on, there is no chance of your daydream becoming anything more than something in your imagination. Your crush exists as an idea in your head; it is nothing else. Still, the feelings associated with having a crush can be similar to feeling like you're in love. But it is unlikely that someone who has never spoken to you will fall in love with you!

When you have a crush on someone, you have choices. You can do nothing, keep

Ways to Get to Know Your Crush

- Have an online chat
- Pass a note
- Talk on the phone
- Have a face-to-face conversation

A Big Crush

your feelings to yourself, and hope that you eventually get over her. Or you can take a chance and do something about your feelings. Most likely you'll feel pretty nervous about what she'll say or do. But if you don't take the chance, you'll never know what her response would have been.

If you decide to let her know you're interested. If you don't know your crush at all, try to become friends first. Start talking to her. Invite her to join a group of friends who are going to the school basketball game. Figure out what common interests you have. For example, if you like listening to the same music or share the same subjects in school, you'll probably find you have plenty to talk about.

If you have a few conversations with a girl before you ask her out, chances are you will be more successful when you do ask her out. If she doesn't know you at all, she may be startled by your invitation. All she'll have to go on is her first impression and the way you look—which may or may not work to your advantage.

Getting to know someone as a friend first can often be rewarding. Conversations between the two of you can be easier.

Running for student council gave Mike an excuse to finally talk to his crush.

And knowing what the other likes to do for fun will help if dating is something you have in mind for the future. And if things don't work out in a romantic relationship, it is possible to go back to being friends if both of you are okay with that.

Does This Crush Have a Chance?

1. Have you had a conversation with this girl?

2. Does she know your name?

3. Do you have any classes with her?

4. Have you ever seen her outside of school?

5. If you answered yes to question 4, did you have a conversation?

6. Do you know how she likes to spend her time?

7. Have you ever talked to her on the phone?

8. Does she come up to you in the hallway to say hello?

Give yourself one point for every "yes."

0-2 = Not a chance

3-5 = Maybe

6-8 = It's looking good

If she's not interested in you. You've tried every trick in the book—carrying her books, walking her to class, holding her spot in the lunch line—and she still won't go out with you. So what do you do?

You could simply try to forget about your crush and move on. Or you could settle for just being her friend. But be honest with yourself and with her—if your feelings for her are more than those of just a friend and she doesn't feel the same way, you probably should not hang around with her until you feel like you can be "just friends."

Getting To Know Her ... Online?

Social networking Web sites such as MySpace and Facebook provide the technology that allows you to make friends around the world. But remember, when you post information online you are making that information available for the whole world to see. If you think certain things should be private, don't put them on the Internet. Strangers might use that information to steal your identity, hack your computer, or even stalk you. Other Internet safety tips include:

- Be extremely careful about talking to and flirting with people you don't know. Some people using the Internet include false information, and they pretend to be someone they are not.

- Restrict access to your Web site to the people you know.

- Don't post your full name, address, phone number, and other private information.

- Remember, once you post information, it may remain available anyway. Others may have saved it to their computers and they can repost it again even if you take it down.

- Be wary of meeting people you've met online in person. If you decide to, meet in a public place during the day with friends. Tell an adult what you are doing before you go. Make sure that person knows where you're going and when you'll be back.

- If you feel threatened by or uncomfortable about something posted about you or someone you know, tell your parents or another adult you trust. Report it to the police and to the social networking site.[1]

Another option is to be patient, and bide your time. Try inviting her to some activities involving a group of your friends. This way, she'll have a chance to get to know you and accept a date once she knows you better. Or maybe you'll find you're no longer interested. But if you are still interested, ask her out again. Just because she said no once doesn't mean she'll say no the second or third time. However, there is a difference between a determined pursuer and a stalker. If she's

What Are My Options?

A. Go for it!

If your crush is on a classmate, try to hang out with her as a friend. Once you start spending time around her, your feelings and ideas will become much clearer. If a romantic relationship doesn't work out, at least you'll get a new friend.

B. Forget about it!

If the crush is unrealistic (like on a celebrity you'll never meet) or if you don't feel ready for a relationship, try to get the person off your mind. Spend your time on a new hobby or sport with your friends.

C. Talk about it.

Pull aside one of your friends and tell him or her what is on your mind. Ask your friend for an opinion or advice about what to do. Make sure you confide in a close friend, who won't tell others about your situation. And if you're the one being confided in, don't gossip about your friend's crush.

Love

If your crush doesn't want to make a decision on dating right away, you can still hang out with her "as friends." There is a chance her feelings may change once she gets to know you better.

already told you to stay out of her way, it's unlikely she'll change her mind about going out with you. Respect her decision and leave her alone.

Some of the time, you will ask a girl out and get flat-out rejected. If she says no, it hurts—a lot. But try to remember, these things happen to people all the time. Being rejected is not the end of the world. To rebound, call some of your guy friends to join in some activities that will keep your mind off of what happened. Play video games, watch a movie, play basketball or football, or listen to your favorite album.

At some point in time you'll find yourself interested in a different girl. And she may be the one who gives you the answer you want to hear. Even if you are unsuccessful, it isn't the worst thing in the world to be friends.

CHAPTER THREE

First Dates

> Brad finally got the courage up to ask Jackie out and she said yes. Now he is worried about what will happen next. Will she like him? Where should they go? A movie is a possibility, and maybe dinner before that. Brad's really worried. What if she doesn't have a good time hanging out with him? Will they ever talk again? He feels unsure of himself and uncertain about what he's gotten into.

Are you ready to start dating? There is really no right time or age when people should start dating. It varies from person to person. Some people have relationships without going out on formal dates, that is, dates with just the two of you. In fact, you may really care about someone whom you see mostly at school or while hanging out with other friends.

Family rules. Actually, the decision to go out on a formal date may not be entirely up to you. Some parents may forbid their kids from dating until they reach a certain age. Others may feel their kids are simply not ready yet—or they may feel uncomfortable about a specific person their kid is interested in dating.

This doesn't refer to just her parents. Your folks may not be comfortable with

Once Jackie said yes, Brad thought the hard part was over. Then he realized he had no plan for their date!

the idea of you dating, either. If that is the case, you may need to take some steps to earn their support. The best way to do that is to show that you are a responsible person in other areas. If your parents ask you to take care of certain chores, make sure you get them done on time and without an argument.

In the same way, you'll want to figure out ways to show the parents of the girl you want to date that you can be trusted. If you really like the person and want to date her, try to get to know her parents. At some point you could ask them why they have those rules. At the very worst, you might not be able to take her on dates, but if the parents meet you and think well of you, they could eventually change their mind. You may have to simply wait for them to say it's okay for her to date you.

If both sets of parents give the okay for you to date, most likely they will establish some rules. One of the biggest ones is the curfew—the time they set for you to be back home after a date. If you want her parents to approve of you—and not object to any future dates—your best bet is to try to abide by the rules they establish. If they want their daughter home by 11:00 P.M., do your best to make sure that happens—or be ready to explain to her parents

Be sure to get your date home by her curfew. And make sure you're home in time for yours.

> "When men and women are able to respect and accept their differences then love has a chance to blossom."
>
> —John Gray

what happened that made you arrive at her home at 11:15 P.M. instead.

Similarly, show your parents that you are responsible by abiding by the curfew they set for you. If you don't agree with their restrictions, ask if you can discuss them further. Have a conversation in which you remain calm and polite. Perhaps they can help you understand where they are coming from. At the same time, you can let them know how you feel about the situation. Perhaps they will change your curfew time. But if they don't, make sure you follow their rules. Don't make them worry about you because you're late. If you show them that you can be responsible, they may be willing to talk about making some changes to family rules and curfews in the future.

Recognize that parents set rules on curfews for their daughters—and sons—because they care about their kids.

First Impressions

If you want her parents to think well of you, be sure to make a good first impression. Be attentive and polite when they are talking to you. While meeting the parents can be potentially embarrassing, just keep in mind that her parents want to know who you are because they care about their daughter. And if they don't like you, they can influence her decision about whether to keep dating you.

They want to know where they are and have them home at a reasonable hour because they want them to be safe.

How parents can help. Depending on how old you are and whether or not you have a driver's license, you may find that you have to depend on her parents or yours to provide transportation on dates. Most states don't allow kids to get their license until the age of sixteen or older. But if you need a ride and the parents are able, they will probably be happy to help out. Be sure to ask them politely and to give some advance notice, too, if possible.

One magazine poll notes that 91 percent of teens say they don't like having a parent driving them around on a date.[1] However, when they don't have an alternative way of getting places, most teens appreciate getting a ride from their mother or father.

When you meet your date's parents, shake her father's hand. Smile, and make eye contact. It doesn't hurt if you dress up a bit, either.

Parents may also be willing to help you out financially on dates. That is why it helps to be on good terms with your folks and to keep them informed about your dating plans. In fact, they would probably also welcome the chance to meet the girl you like. If they can help out, parents are more likely to offer some cash for you to use on a date if they know your plans.

Another way parents can help is by talking to you about dating and relationships. Take a few minutes to ask for advice or their opinion about the person you are interested in dating. You'll be showing them that you value their advice, and you may also gain some new perspectives.

The first date. First dates can be intimidating, although your comfort level may depend on how well you know your date before asking her out and how much time you have already spent together. If you have not had many conversations with the girl until now, you may find it hard to talk in a one-on-one setting.

Three Approaches to Try When Asking for a Date

The direct approach: Go up to the girl and just ask, "Will you go out with me?" Simple and easy.

The conversational approach: Start a conversation by talking about things she is interested in or about something that happened in class. During the conversation, slip in a suggestion that you both go to the movies.

The long-term approach: Have several friendly conversations with the girl. Ask her different things. Discuss her interests. Build a casual friendship. Then, when you feel comfortable enough, ask her out on a date.[2]

When You Ask Her Out

Get to know her first. If asking her out are the first words you have said to her, then chances are you may not be successful.

Have a plan. Know what you are going to say and where the date will be.

Speak clearly. It can be hard to talk when you're feeling nervous, but do you want her to have to ask you to repeat yourself? Don't mumble—make sure you talk so that she can understand you.

Act confident, even if you don't really feel confident. Girls don't want to go out with a guy who seems nervous and unsure of himself.

No matter how well you know her, there's a lot you can do to make a good impression. Be respectful and polite. Open doors, give her compliments, and treat her well.

At the same time, be aware of how she treats you. If she appears to take your attention as something she deserves, but doesn't treat you with any respect in return, you might want to reconsider your interest in her. Similarly, you'll want to notice how she treats other people. Is she rude when you introduce her to the

Surprise your date with flowers. This will make a great first impression on her.

friend you meet at the movie theater? Does she make mean comments about the waitress in the restaurant? The little things that she does on your first date can tell you a lot.

Some First Date Do's and Don'ts

DO make eye contact. Be sure to look her in the eye while you are talking. It will make it easier for both of you to talk.

DO relax. Take it easy and let the date progress. Don't try to be someone else or to be a comedian (unless you really are one). Act natural.

DO compliment her. Say nice things to her. Compliment her dress and appearance.

DO spontaneous things. Don't be shy about changing plans for your date if an idea pops in your head.

DON'T be pushy. Don't be too physical. A little bit of contact isn't bad, but don't try to hold her hand—or do anything else!—if it makes her uncomfortable.

DON'T talk only about yourself. Get her to talk about herself by asking a lot of questions that keep the conversation moving.

DON'T limit your date. Keep an open mind. If at first she doesn't seem quite what you had in mind, give her a chance. You may be surprised!

DON'T use swear words. There isn't anything more unattractive than a guy who swears a lot.[3]

Great First Dates

Here are some fun things to do on a first date:

The classic date—The dinner and a movie gig is the go-to first date for a lot of people. However, it can be expensive and require transportation. You can always invite her over to your house for a pizza and a movie that you rented. Make sure it is one that she likes and that she and her parents know that your parents will be home.

The researched date—Talk to her friends and find out some of her interests. If she likes playing a sport, take her somewhere where the two of you can compete. Don't be afraid if she's better than you. After all, fun—not winning—is the point.

The creative date—Think up some fun activities such as a walk through a local art museum, a hike in the woods, or a game of Frisbee in the park.

During your date, talk and ask questions. This is your opportunity to learn more about her. You may find that the feelings of attraction that initially drew you to her can fizzle out quickly if you have very little in common. On the other hand, even if you have many differences, you may decide that this makes her very interesting.

Remember, a date is an opportunity to get to know someone better. Don't put unnecessary pressures on yourself or your date. Relax and have fun.

CHAPTER FOUR

The Dating Game

> *Each night, Tim and Melissa talk on the phone for an hour. Every weekend they go to the movies together or they meet at each other's houses to watch a DVD together. One day a week they both volunteer at the animal shelter. Because they live close to each other, they often take walks in the evenings after dinner.*

Spending time with a girl gives you the chance **to really know her.** The more time you spend with her, for example, the better idea you have of what she is like

when she is mad, stressed, upset, or happy. You'll know what she likes to do for fun and what dreams and desires she has.

Over time, you may find there are things that you really admire and appreciate in your girlfriend. Or you may find that as you get to know her better, there are certain things that you don't like or approve of. In other words, after a certain period of time, you know enough about yourself and about her to determine if you would like to stay in the relationship.

Things to do. While you're still in the "getting to know you" stage, you don't have to go out on formal dates all the time. You can see each other when you get together with friends or just hang out with each other. Some informal dates can include the following:

- Attend school plays, music program concerts, and sporting events together.

- Put together a basket of food and go for a picnic in the park or in her backyard.

- Go on a walk around the neighborhood. This can give you some privacy and quality time together.

- Teach her a sport you like to play or ask her to teach you one that she enjoys.

- Or if you don't play sports, think of something else you could work on together. Teach her your favorite video game or work on creating a Web site together.

- Volunteer together at an animal shelter or nursing home.

Who pays? In the beginning of a dating relationship, the person who did the asking out should cover the costs of the date. But after you have been going out together for a while, it's okay to talk about who pays for dates that are expensive. Seeing movies or going to concerts can cost a lot. Let her know if things are getting too expensive for you. Maybe she'll offer to pay for tickets. Make sure you

"It doesn't matter if the guy is perfect or the girl is perfect, as long as they are perfect for each other."

—from the 1997 film *Good Will Hunting*

An inexpensive date can be a picnic by a lake or at an outdoor music concert.

have enough money on you to cover likely expenses before you go out on a date.

Make her feel special. If you have been together for awhile, you may want to show her that you really appreciate her. There are a lot of little ways you can share your romantic feelings.

You could play music that reminds you both of your first dance together or your first date. A lot of couples will have a special song that they refer to as "Our Song," whenever they hear it played.

Let Her Know You Care

Here are some silly one-liners that will make her smile:

"Are you tired? Because you've been running through my mind all day."

"If I were to rearrange the alphabet I would put U and I together."

"Help, something's wrong with my eyes! I just can't take mine off you."

"You're like a dictionary—you add meaning to my life!"

"Do you have a map? 'Cause I just got lost in your eyes."

When your girlfriend is upset about something, be there to give her a hug and a shoulder to cry on. You don't really need to say anything at all. Just let her know you'll be around when she's feeling down.

During the year, remember the monthly anniversary of your first date. Write a note, send a card, give her chocolates, or pick some flowers and present her with the bouquet. Make sure not to forget her birthday and the big one-year anniversary.

If she gets sick, come by for a visit with a big get-well card that all your friends signed. You could also bring a big balloon or some flowers. It will make her feel so much better to know that you care.

Dating Manners

1. Be on time.
2. Be polite.
3. Be thoughtful.
4. Be honest.
5. Be flexible.[1]

Remember your anniversary by marking it on your calendar!

CHAPTER FIVE

Making Things Work

> John and Lindsey have been dating for about six months. After spending a lot of time together, both in and out of school, they have gotten to know each other pretty well. John knows that when Lindsey is stressed out, she will sometimes snap at him. Lindsey sees that John often deals with his problems by ignoring them, and sometimes that includes her. They both realize that these habits are not the best way to deal with each other and are working to try to change.

When you're in love with someone, you do your best to keep your relationship strong. In John and Lindsey's case, they are aware they have some problems with how they sometimes treat each other. However, both are making an effort to do something about it.

A serious relationship is more than sexual attraction. It requires taking a strong interest in the other person. You both need to think about what you need to do to keep things strong. The best relationships—including those with friends and family—involve four important elements: trust, honesty, respect, and good communication.

Trust. An important part of a healthy relationship is being able to trust the other person. That means you both can believe that the other will be reliable. You both consider your commitment to each other to be serious. That means you'll do your best to be there for each other, especially during stressful times. And you'll consider your relationship of major importance. That means neither of you will risk losing it by flirting with other people. If there is a lack of trust between the two of you, your relationship is headed for problems.

Honesty. Related to trust, honesty is essential to any good, healthy relationship. If you aren't telling your girlfriend the truth, then she'll never be able to trust anything you say. Along these lines, don't pretend to be someone you're not or to be interested in certain things that she likes if you really aren't. Of course, you should make an effort to learn about her interests before stating that you don't like them. But if you can't be willing and open to learning about what she likes, perhaps the two of you aren't a good match.

Respect. To respect someone means to pay attention and give value to the feelings, rights, and wishes of that person. In other words, it means treating the other person as you would like to be treated yourself. After you've spent a lot of time

Give your girlfriend her space. You don't need to phone her when her plans don't include you.

Being honest may sound simple, but sometimes it can be hard to practice. You may not want to talk with your girlfriend about what is on your mind and how you are feeling. Most guys have trouble doing that, but do your best to make your honest opinions part of your relationship.

with a person, you may find you're taking her for granted. Or worse, you may fall into a habit of teasing or insulting her. No one deserves that kind of treatment. If you can't be respectful in your relationships, you may soon lose them.

Along the same lines, in a relationship with a girl, it is important to respect her wishes when it comes to the physical aspect of love. It is up to you to have respect for her feelings and comfort level. Don't pressure her to do things she wouldn't normally want to do.

Good communication. When you care about someone, you should always strive to share your thoughts. Communicating can mean simply letting each other know your plans for the week, or it can mean talking about why one of you is angry with the other.

Sometimes issues will come up: She may get jealous that you were talking to another girl, or you may feel jealous of her. She may get angry, thinking you want to hang out with your friends more than with her. Or

When you have a disagreement, make sure you talk face-to-face rather than through cell phones.

maybe you're upset that you haven't seen her for a long time because she's been "too busy."

These kinds of situations can lead to serious disagreements that could endanger your relationship. To keep it strong, you both need to try to solve your misunderstandings and conflicts in healthy ways.

This means you need to bring up the problem in a direct way, but without placing any blame. Let her know that you think she

Ingredients for a Successful and Loving Relationship

1. **Attraction** is the "chemistry" part of love. It's all about the physical interest that two people have in each other. Attraction is responsible for the desire you feel to kiss and hold the object of your affection. Attraction is also what's behind the flushed, nervous-but-excited way you feel when that person is near.

2. **Closeness** is the bond that develops when you share thoughts and feelings that you don't share with anyone else. When you have this feeling of closeness with the person you are dating, you feel supported, cared for, understood, and accepted for who you are. Trust is a big part of this.

3. **Commitment** is the promise or decision to stick by the other person through the ups and downs of the relationship.[1]

has been mean to you, or ask if you have done something to upset her. The next step is to talk about how it makes you feel. Does it make you mad that she didn't talk to you all day? Or is she angry that you were out with your friends and didn't call her at all?

Try to be open and not react with anger or other negative emotions when listening to her side of the story. If you are at

Dinner with the Parents

She invites you over to her house for dinner with her family. A panic comes over you. What do you do? Here are a few tips:

Dress well. Avoid sneakers and sandals. If the weather is cold, wear a good sweater.

Always say "please" and "thank you" when asking for dishes.

Look family members in the eye when you are talking to them.

Be yourself.

Offer to help clear the table or serve dessert.

Make sure you treat your girlfriend well.

fault, apologize and try to find out what you can do in order to make it up to her. Say something like, "I'm really sorry about what I did. I didn't know it would make you feel that way."

If you think she did something wrong, choose your words carefully. Let her know how her behavior made you feel: "I felt upset when I didn't hear from you all day because I thought something happened to you." That kind of statement works a lot better in clearing the air than making an angry, accusatory statement like "Why didn't you call?!"

> ### Characteristics of a Healthy Relationship
>
> * Strong interest in each other as persons
> * Mutual respect
> * Trust
> * Honesty
> * Support
> * Fairness and equality
> * Separate identities
> * Good communication[2]

Remember, the way you communicate can go a long way to resolving problems. The way you handle your disagreements and arguments says a lot about how much you trust and respect each other.

Always try to solve your problems. Don't ignore or walk away, unless you need a few moments to get a handle on your angry feelings. Dealing with conflicts in a relationship is difficult. However, if you are willing to put time into figuring out how to resolve them, then your relationship will not only survive, but it will grow stronger.

CHAPTER SIX

Your Other Relationships

It was Friday night and Michael had a problem. He was supposed to go to his girlfriend Natalie's house and keep her company while she babysat her little sister. But his friend Nick had just called him to say that the guys were going to the basketball courts to play a pickup game under the lights. Michael's friends gave him a hard time yesterday because he had already spent most of that week hanging out with Natalie. He didn't want to make his friends even madder, but he also knew that Natalie would not be happy if he bailed on her.

Even when you're in a committed relationship, it is important that you don't forget your other relationships. Of course, if you've made a promise to help your girlfriend out with a chore, you need to abide by that promise. But if no promises were made, you shouldn't feel guilty about wanting to do stuff with friends sometimes. And she shouldn't get mad that your parents say you can't go out with her this weekend because they want you to visit your grandmother. After all, other people are a part of your life, too.

Making time for friends. While a romantic relationship can be fun and you can enjoy

Michael has to choose between his friends and his girlfriend. What should he do?

spending a lot of time with the girl you are dating, you don't need to give her your exclusive attention. Some people have lost friends when dating because they haven't made time for anyone else.

Discovering the balance between time spent with your girlfriend and with your group of friends can be difficult. Both deserve a certain amount of attention. You don't want your friends to be mad at you for spending too much time with your girlfriend. But at the same time, you don't want your girlfriend to be angry that you're always with the guys.

Be aware of the message you're sending when you ignore the group or the girl—one or the other will come to believe the relationship doesn't mean much to you. And think about it. What happens if you and your girlfriend break up? If you have drifted away from your friends, you will have lost an important support group. You need to make sure to maintain a healthy balance between your group of friends and your girlfriend.

Dealing with teasing. Maybe you've started dating earlier than a lot of your friends. Now they're giving you a

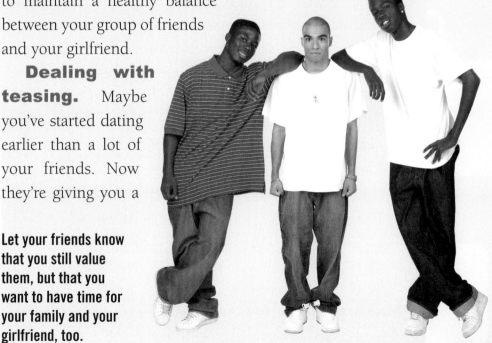

Let your friends know that you still value them, but that you want to have time for your family and your girlfriend, too.

"Love is a choice you make from moment to moment."

—Barbara De Angelis

hard time when you tell them you're going to watch your girlfriend's basketball game instead of joining them for a video game session.

Do your best to accept that there will be teasing from your friends. Their behavior is normal. They may be envious of you and your relationship. Or in their way, they may be saying they're hurt that you don't want to spend time with them. Whatever is behind their remarks, they are still your friends.

Just smile and do your best to ignore the teasing. But don't distance yourself from friends. Make sure you set aside times when you do things with just them. Invite them over or suggest a pickup game for next weekend. Do your best to keep those relationships alive.

An even more difficult form of teasing may come from your family. Both younger and older brothers and sisters may tease you for being "in love." Or they may do their best to embarrass you in front of your girlfriend.

Teasing from siblings can be harder to deal with than that from friends, because you can't always walk away from it. Try not to show it if you feel annoyed. Leave the situation—go to your room or take a walk. Don't let yourself be brought down by their teasing. However, if it gets to be too much, let your mother or father know, and ask for some advice on what to do. It's likely your parents will listen to your complaint and have a talk with the troublemakers.

Making time for family. Parents can sometimes become annoyed when you spend every waking hour with your new love and overlook your responsibilities at home. They may also be concerned if you are never available for family activities.

Avoid these kinds of issues by keeping communication lines open with your mother and father. You can keep your parents happy by letting them know your plans. For example, before you call your girlfriend to say you'll be over on Saturday afternoon, make sure your father knows that you're counting on him to give you a ride. Double check with your mother about when the party for your uncle's fiftieth birthday party is so you don't ask your girl to a movie that night. In other words, keep your parents in the loop. Do your best to communicate with them.

Set aside time to be with your family and friends. Don't bail on them whenever your girlfriend calls.

If your parents decide you shouldn't date each other. Perhaps her parents just don't like you. Or maybe your parents don't like her, and they forbid you from seeing each other anymore. What do you do?

It is a serious matter when your parents don't like the person you are dating because she is of a different background, race, or religion. A situation like this can be an opportunity to sit down and talk to your parents about what they believe and why they believe it. Even if you feel angry about their attitude, keep a level head and explain why you disagree.

On the other hand, perhaps your parents don't like your new girlfriend because they don't like the way she treats you. Their opinion should cause you to think seriously about the relationship that you are in.

Letting your parents influence your decisions can be hard. But when it comes to a relationship with the opposite sex, what your parents think and want can have a big influence over whether or not you hang out with a specific

If your parents don't want you to see your girlfriend, hear them out. If you don't agree, talk to them.

Talk to Your Parents

Discuss the rules ahead of time so you are clear about their expectations.

Follow the rules. If your plans mean you'll be late for curfew, let them know and ask if you can have an exception to the rule.

Pick your battles. Avoid fights over every little thing. If you are going to argue, make sure you deal with the issues that are important to you.

Don't lose your temper. Try to remain calm when your parents say no about something. Listen to what they say.

In a calm voice, ask to explain your side of the issue. Ask your parents to give you the same respect that they want from you.

Accept their decision gracefully, even if it is not the response you wanted.

person. Ask yourself: "Is this girl worth getting into a fight with my parents?"

If you continue seeing this girl despite what your parents say, they will only become angry. You will have broken their trust by sneaking around behind their back. And a broken trust is hard to repair.

The best thing to do if your parents want you to end a relationship is to sit down with them and have a long discussion. Try to find out their specific reasons. But be willing to compromise—maybe you and the girl in question may only be friends for now. In time, your folks may change their mind. But meanwhile, respect their point of view.

CHAPTER SEVEN

Do the Right Thing

> *Trent and Michelle have been dating for around three months. They hang out all day after school, watch movies together, and see each other for weekend dates. Since Michelle and Trent are going out, she doesn't think he should be having anything to do with other girls. The other day she saw him talking with Julie, one of his friends from class. Michelle became furious. She cornered Trent later that day and let him know that he shouldn't be talking to other girls.*

Is it love or is it jealousy? Michelle is acting jealous and putting demands on Trent that he doesn't think are fair at all. Her behavior makes him wonder about whether to stay with her.

What do you do when you really care about someone but you don't think the person is treating you right? One of the worst things to do is nothing—thinking that if you just ignore her outbursts, they'll eventually stop. Ignoring a problem

Michelle's jealous outbursts are taking their toll on Trent. Should he stop talking to other girls or break it off with Michelle?

won't solve it. When you both don't agree about something, you need to take steps to solve the conflict. That means you need to talk. In Michelle's case, she needs to recognize she has a problem—her jealousy is not a sign of her love. It is a sign of controlling and unhealthy behavior.

When jealousy becomes abuse. When one partner in a relationship is jealous and controlling, things can quickly go from bad to worse. Such problems occur in as many as one out of three teen relationships, some studies show.[1] The vast majority of cases involve the boy being abusive to his girlfriend.[2] This abuse can be controlling behavior in which the guy puts down and constantly criticizes the girl, blames her for his problems, or uses threats of violence or actual violence.

If you have a friend who is in an abusive relationship, try to get help for that person. Talk with someone you trust—a teacher, a guidance counselor, a doctor, a friend, or a parent. You may also want to contact the police

Be aware that your jealous feelings can affect your relationship.

or call one of the crisis or domestic violence hotlines listed on page 61. If the person wants to stay in the relationship, he or she must realize that the violence will not go away by itself. Counseling or some other form of outside help is necessary.

Just because you feel jealous from time to time doesn't mean you are abusive and controlling. But watch yourself. If you find yourself feeling jealous of your girlfriend, stop and think. Be aware that your jealous feelings are affecting your behavior and the way you treat her. Remember, love means being respectful and caring in a relationship.

Respect her and respect yourself. Respect is a key part of any relationship. In friendships, it means that good friends respect your values and beliefs. They don't tease or put you down because you stand by your choices, like in making decisions about whether to smoke cigarettes or drink alcohol. It is important to resist peer pressure to do things you don't think are right or that you aren't comfortable with.

An Unhealthy Relationship?

You are in an unhealthy relationship if your girlfriend . . .

. . . Constantly criticizes the way you look or dress.

. . . Keeps you from seeing friends or from talking to any other guys or girls.

. . . Wants you to quit an activity, even though you love it, so you can spend more time with her.

. . . Hits you whenever she's angry.[3]

Are You Treating Her Right?

Take this quiz to see if you are treating your girlfriend right. Give yourself one point for every yes answer and zero points for each no answer.

1. Do you get jealous when you see your girlfriend talking to other boys (who are her friends)?

2. Do you insist that your girlfriend call you every day?

3. If your girlfriend doesn't walk with you between classes, does that make you upset?

4. Have you ever yelled or raised your voice at your girlfriend?

5. Have you ever hit or threatened to hit your girlfriend?

6. Do you get jealous when your girlfriend spends time with her friends and isn't hanging out with you?

7. Do you say mean or nasty things to your girlfriend if she doesn't hang out with you?

8. Have you ever made your girlfriend do something she said no to repeatedly?

If you scored less than 2, your relationship is in good shape.

If you scored 3-5, then your relationship may not be healthy.

If you scored 6-8, then check yourself. You are not treating your girlfriend right. If you have concerns about your behavior, you may want to ask for help from a guidance counselor or another trusted adult.

If you're in a serious relationship, it is also possible that your friends are influencing your decisions about having a physical relationship with your girlfriend. Even if your friends aren't pressuring you, you're getting the message from the media—whether TV, film, or Internet—which are saturated with images and stories focusing on sex and seduction. Studies have shown that teens exposed to heavy sexual content in the media are twice as likely to engage in a sexual relationship.[4]

Sexually Transmitted Diseases (STDs)

When untreated, STDs can lead to infertility (the inability to father children) and even death. Here are the six most common STDs in men.

AIDS: A viral disease that attacks and wears down the immune system. Acquired immune deficiency syndrome (AIDS) is caused by the human immunodeficiency virus (HIV).

Chlamydia: An infection caused by the bacterium *Chlamydia trachomatis.*

Genital herpes: A viral infection caused by the herpes simplex virus (HSV) that can cause blisters and sores.

Gonorrhea: An infection caused by the bacterium *Neisseria gonorrhoeae.*

Human papillomavirus (HPV): A virus that can cause genital warts and increase the risk of various cancers.

Syphilis: An infection caused by the bacterium *Treponema pallidum.*[5]

Boundaries should be established between the two of you before any physical contact is made. Tell one another what you're comfortable with.

Any kind of sexual activity should be treated very seriously. Being sexually active can lead to all kinds of serious consequences—from pregnancy to sexually transmitted diseases (STDs) to emotional problems. Condoms are a form of contraception that can help prevent pregnancy as well as some STDs; however, they are not 100 percent effective. Be careful, and remember that the safest sex is abstinence—not having sex at all. If you need more information, you may want to speak to your parents, a health teacher or guidance counselor, a doctor, or another trusted adult.

In a good relationship, your girlfriend will understand and accept your values and beliefs. So make sure you talk to her about how you feel and why you feel that way. Remember, you have to make the choice to do what seems right to you.

Endings and Beginnings

Ben was devastated. His girlfriend of two years, Lucille, had just dumped him. They had started dating when they were in eighth grade. They would go to the park, watch movies, take walks, and play basketball. He had his first kiss with her. But recently, Lucille had started acting differently when she was around Ben. She didn't have time to stop to talk when he saw her in the hallway. And she often seemed irritated and angry with him. But yesterday was the worst—Lucille had texted him two fateful words: "It's over."

When Ben's girlfriend dumped him, it really hurt. And it hurt even more because she chose an unfair way to break up. Anyone who has been in a serious relationship with another person deserves to be told face-to-face when it's over. If the dumper hides behind technology, the dumpee not only feels rejected, but insulted as well. His first thought is likely to be, "So that's how much our relationship meant to her?"

When she breaks up with you. The first thing to do is accept that the other person has reached a point in her life in which she's decided she doesn't want to date you anymore. People change. You can't control how your girl thinks about you after a few months or even years of being in a close relationship. If

It's Over!!

she doesn't feel the same way about you anymore, that doesn't mean you are worthless or that she is cruel. Change happens.

The second thing to do is to not hold on to false hope that she will change her mind and decide to come back. If she has reached the point of saying that it's over, it probably is. What you need to do is recognize that the best thing for you is to let go and move on.

When you break things off. When things don't feel right anymore, it could be time for you to end the relationship. While dealing with being dumped by your girlfriend is hard, it can be just as challenging to break up with her. This requires you to be open and honest, while recognizing that you might be hurting her feelings.

> "The hottest love has the coldest end."
>
> —Socrates

Some Reasons for Breaking Up

- She's cheated on you.
- She's disrespectful of you, often insulting you or putting you down.
- You've grown apart, and you no longer want to spend your time with her.
- You have different goals that won't allow you to stay together.

You need to let her know when things between you aren't right.

Making the decision to break it off can be hard. In some cases, it may be as simple as not having strong feelings for your girlfriend. Or you recognize that there is something about her that you can't stand. Whatever the reason, it is in the best interest of both of you to end the relationship. There is no good reason to remain in a relationship that leaves both of you unhappy. Having to break up with someone, while difficult, will make you become a stronger person.

The best advice to follow when breaking up with a girl is to be sensitive. Think to

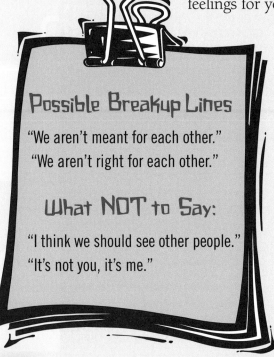

Possible Breakup Lines

"We aren't meant for each other."
"We aren't right for each other."

What NOT to Say:

"I think we should see other people."
"It's not you, it's me."

yourself, "How would I like to be treated in this situation?" If you put yourself in the shoes of your girlfriend and have that attitude, you will be able to let her down easy and possibly become friends one day.

Other tips for a breakup include making sure that it is done in private. Don't dump her in a restaurant surrounded by a group of people. It could get ugly. But make sure that you break up with her to her face; don't use any kind of Internet messaging service or a text message. In the same way, breaking up over the phone, rather than face-to-face, is wrong.

Honesty is the best policy when breaking up with a girl. If you don't feel the same attraction you did for your girlfriend, the fair thing to do for her is to break up. Staying in a relationship with someone because she is still interested in you, but you really aren't, is unfair. Coming clean and letting her know why you think it needs to end is the only way to have a "good" breakup.

Tips for Making a Clean Break

DO	Give her a legitimate reason why you want to end the relationship.
DO	Break up with her face-to-face.
DON'T	Break up with her via text message, instant message, or e-mail.
DON'T	Break up with her over the phone.
DON'T	Come up with some flimsy excuse.

When it comes time to have "the talk," make sure you choose somewhere private where both of you will have the opportunity to say what's really on your minds.

For the most part, breakups can be messy. In the worst-case scenario, you never talk to her again. Other cases may not be as bad, and you may end up becoming good friends.

Feeling depressed after a breakup. Whether it was your decision or hers, you can feel really sad after a breakup. The painful feelings of loss can overwhelm you with strong emotions, including anger, sorrow, grief, and depression.

However, be aware that if negative thoughts and feelings of depression persist for more than two weeks, you may be suffering from a mental disorder known as clinical depression. Its symptoms include feelings of extreme sadness and hopelessness, an inability to concentrate, feelings of guilt, and thoughts of death. Suicide among teens commonly occurs following a stressful life event—and that includes a breakup with a boyfriend or girlfriend. The third-leading cause of death among fifteen- to twenty-five-year-olds is suicide.[1] In 2004, 82 percent of all suicides ages ten to twenty-four were boys.[2]

If you're worried that a friend is depressed or possibly suicidal, you need to get help for that person. Share your concerns with an adult—your parents, a school counselor, your family doctor, or a religious leader. You could also contact a suicide prevention hotline—see the hotline telephone numbers listed on page 61.

Moving on and starting over. Moving on after a painful breakup can be a difficult process, especially if the breakup wasn't your idea. What's important is to try to stay strong and take care of yourself. Try to eat well and get plenty of sleep. Go out for a run or get some other kind of exercise. There is nothing like a good run to take your mind off of something and help you feel good about yourself.

The time right after a breakup can be the hardest. Depending on how close you had grown to your ex-girlfriend, you may have a whole lot of free time. This can be both good and bad. Fill the hours by getting together with friends. Or pick up a new activity or hobby to help keep your mind off of her.

Push yourself to act like you're okay, even if you're feeling terrible. Try not to be hard on yourself. If she was the one who broke up

Symptoms of Clinical Depression

- A loss of interest in activities previously enjoyed
- Feelings of worthlessness or guilt
- Fatigue or loss of energy
- Withdrawal from friends and family
- Sudden decline in grades
- Appetite or weight changes

Tips for Getting Over a Breakup

Take care of yourself physically: Get enough sleep, eat healthy foods, and exercise regularly.

Don't focus your thoughts on what happened: Don't just sit around the house and feel sorry for yourself. Instead, try to think about other possibilities in your life. Set new goals for yourself and your future.

Think about your good qualities: Getting dumped will leave your self-esteem at a new low. Take some time to think about or even write down some of your positive characteristics.

Do the things you normally enjoy: Go and enjoy a favorite activity, whether it's a sport or a good book. Hang out with some friends and try to forget the girl.

Share your feelings: Sit down with a trusted friend or with a parent and talk about what you are going through. It will feel good to get your problems off your chest.

Give yourself time: You won't get over the girl right away. Allow for time to heal your wounds.

with you, keep reminding yourself that the breakup was not your fault. It wasn't something you said or did wrong. Sometimes, as people grow older, they realize they want something different in a relationship. There are other girls out there who will appreciate you. Stay positive and hold on to your self-respect and self-confidence.

Try to go through the motions during your day-to-day life, even though it can be hard. Keep telling yourself, "It's not the end of the world. Things will get better." In time, they really will get better. You just have to give yourself time.

Whatever you do, don't look to jump into a new relationship right way. Take some time off before trying to date someone again. But don't let that stop you from getting to know new people and making new friends. Eventually, you'll get over that old relationship and one of those new friends might begin to mean something special to you.

While romantic relationships can be one of the most challenging and confusing parts of life, they can also be the most rewarding. During the emotional highs and lows of crushes and romances, you have the chance to grow and learn how to be the best for yourself and for others.

Having fun with good friends is a surefire way to keep your mind off your romantic troubles.

CHAPTER NOTES

Chapter 1. This Thing Called Love

1. Lauren Slater, "Love," *National Geographic*, February 2006, p. 49.

Chapter 2. A Big Crush

1. Adapted from "Facts for Consumers: Social Networking Sites: Safety Tips for Tweens and Teens," *Federal Trade Commission*, May 2006, <http://www.ftc.gov/bcp/edu/pubs/consumer/tech/tec14.shtm> (April 27, 2008).

Chapter 3. First Dates

1. "Trend Poll," *Teen People*, March 2002.

2. Adapted from Susan Rabens, *The Complete Idiot's Guide to Dating for Teens* (Indianapolis, Ind.: Alpha, 2001), pp. 62–67.

3. Adapted from Lindsay, "Ten Do's & Don'ts on a First Date," *Helpingteens.org*, May 19, 2007, <http://www.helpingteens.org/article-0124.html> (April 27, 2008).

Chapter 4. The Dating Game

1. Cherie Burbach, "First Date Etiquette," *Suite101.com*, May 15, 2007, <http://dating.suite101.com/article.cfm/basic_dating_etiquette> (April 27, 2008).

Chapter 5. Making Things Work

1. Adapted from "Love & Romance," *TeensHealth*, February 2007, <http://www.kidshealth.org/teen/your_mind/relationships/love.html> (April 28, 2008).

2. Adapted from "Am I in a Healthy Relationship?" *TeensHealth*, April 2008, <http://www.kidshealth.org/teen/your_mind/relationships/healthy_relationship.html> (April 28, 2008).

Chapter 7. Do the Right Thing

1. "Teens and Dating Abuse," *The National Domestic Violence Hotline*, n.d., <http://www.ndvh.org/educate/teen.html> (April 28, 2008).

2. Ibid.

3. Adapted from "Am I in a Healthy Relationship?" *TeensHealth*, April 2008, <http://www.kidshealth.org/teen/your_mind/relationships/healthy_relationship.html> (April 28, 2008).

4. "Media May Prompt Teen Sex," *CBS News*, April 3, 2006, <http://www.cbsnews.com/stories/2006/04/03/health/webmd/main1464262.shtml> (April 27, 2008).

5. Peter Jaret, "The 6 Most Common STDs in Men," *WebMD*, n.d., <http://men.webmd.com/guide/6-most-common-std-men?page=1> (April 29, 2008).

Chapter 8. Endings and Beginnings

1. "Suicide Prevention: Youth Suicide," *Centers for Disease Control and Prevention*, September 6, 2007, <http://www.cdc.gov/ncipc/dvp/Suicide/youthsuicide.htm2> (April 27, 2008).

2. Ibid.

abstinence—The practice of refraining from sex.

clinical depression—A mental disorder in which feelings of sadness, hopelessness, and loss of interest in life persist for more than two weeks.

compromise—To settle a disagreement by both sides agreeing to give up something.

contraception—The intentional prevention of pregnancy.

crush—A brief but intense infatuation with someone.

curfew—The designated time a parent sets for a teen to be home.

depression—Strong feelings of sadness and hopelessness.

dopamine—A neurotransmitter associated with pleasurable sensations.

hormone—A chemical substance that signals certain cells of the body to take certain action.

infatuation—An intense, but brief passion or admiration for someone.

love—An intense feeling of caring for another person.

neurotransmitter—A chemical substance in the brain that transmits messages that affect the rest of the body.

peer—A person who is about the same age and often has similar interests.

peer pressure—Influence from one's peers, or people who are the same age.

puberty—The developmental stage of life during which the human body is maturing to adulthood. In boys, puberty generally starts between the ages of ten and fifteen.

social networking site—A Web site where a user creates a personal profile and connects to the profiles of other users.

STD—Sexually transmitted disease; an infection spread by having intercourse with an infected individual.

FURTHER READING

Fox, Annie, and Elizabeth Verdick. *The Teen Survival Guide to Dating & Relating: Real-World Advice on Guys, Girls, Growing Up, and Getting Along.* Minneapolis, Minn.: Free Spirit Publishing, 2005.

Packer, Alex J. *The How Rude! Handbook of Friendship & Dating Manners for Teens: Surviving the Social Scene.* Minneapolis, Minn.: Free Spirit Publishing, 2004.

Pfeifer, Kate Gruenwald. American Medical Association *Boy's Guide to Becoming a Teen.* San Francisco, Calif.: Jossey-Bass, The American Medical Association, 2006.

INTERNET ADDRESSES

DiscoveryHealth: Teen Relationships
http://health.discovery.com/centers/teen/relationships/relationships.html

Nemours Foundation: TeensHealth: Your Mind
http://www.kidshealth.org/teen/your_mind/

Teen Relationships
http://www.teenrelationships.org

HOTLINE TELEPHONE NUMBERS

National Domestic Violence Hotline
1-800-799-SAFE (1-800-799-7233)

The Youth Crisis Hotline
1-800-HIT-HOME (1-800-448-4663)

National Suicide Prevention Lifeline
1-800-273-TALK (1-800-273-8255)

CONTRIBUTORS

Author John Logan is a freelance writer living outside Philadelphia. He has written for various publications on subjects ranging from sports to politics to relationships.

Series advisor Dr. Carroll Izard is the Trustees Distinguished Professor of Psychology at the University of Delaware. His research and writing focuses on the development of emotion knowledge and emotion regulation and their contributions to social and emotional competence. He is author or editor of seventeen books (one of which won a national award) and more than one hundred articles in scientific journals. Dr. Izard is a fellow of both national psychological associations and the American Association for the Advancement of Science. He is the winner of the American Psychological Association's G. Stanley Hall Award and an international exchange fellowship from the National Academy of Sciences.

A Guys' Guide to Anger; A Girls' Guide to Anger
ISBN-13: 978-0-7660-2853-1   ISBN-10: 0-7660-2853-4

A Guys' Guide to Conflict; A Girls' Guide to Conflict
ISBN-13: 978-0-7660-2852-4   ISBN-10: 0-7660-2852-6

A Guys' Guide to Jealousy; A Girls' Guide to Jealousy
ISBN-13: 978-0-7660-2854-8   ISBN-10: 0-7660-2854-2

A Guys' Guide to Loneliness; A Girls' Guide to Loneliness
ISBN-13: 978-0-7660-2856-2   ISBN-10: 0-7660-2856-9

A Guys' Guide to Love; A Girls' Guide to Love
ISBN-13: 978-0-7660-2855-5   ISBN-10: 0-7660-2855-0

A Guys' Guide to Stress; A Girls' Guide to Stress
ISBN-13: 978-0-7660-2857-9   ISBN-10: 0-7660-2857-7

GIRLS!

STOP

Boring Guys' Stuff
From This Point On!

FLIP-iT-OVER
GUIDES TO TEEN EMOTIONS

A Girls' Guide to

Love

Dorothy Kavanaugh

Enslow Publishers, Inc.
40 Industrial Road
Box 398
Berkeley Heights, NJ 07922
USA

http://www.enslow.com

Library of Congress Cataloging-in-Publication Data

Logan, John.
  A guys' guide to love / John Logan. A girls' guide to love / Dorothy Kavanaugh.
     p. cm. — (Flip-it-over guides to teen emotions)
  No collective t.p.; titles transcribed from individual title pages.
  A guys' guide to love and A girls' guide to love will be published together in a reversible-book format.
  Includes bibliographical references and index.
  ISBN-13: 978-0-7660-2855-5 (alk. paper)
  ISBN-10: 0-7660-2855-0 (alk. paper)
  1. Interpersonal relations in adolescence—Juvenile literature. 2. Emotions in adolescence.
3. Teenage boys—Psychology—Juvenile literature. 4. Teenage girls—Psychology—Juvenile
literature. 5. Love—Juvenile literature. I. Kavanaugh, Dorothy, 1969- Girls' guide to love. II. Title.
III. Title: Girls' guide to love.
  BF724.3.I58L64 2008
  155.42'4241—dc22

                                        2008007665

Printed in the United States of America.

10 9 8 7 6 5 4 3 2 1

Produced by OTTN Publishing, Stockton, N.J.

To Our Readers: We have done our best to make sure all Internet Addresses in this book were active and appropriate when we went to press. However, the author and the publisher have no control over and assume no liability for the material available on those Internet sites or on other Web sites they may link to. Any comments or suggestions can be sent by e-mail to comments@enslow.com or to the address on the title page.

♻ Enslow Publishers, Inc., is committed to printing our books on recycled paper. The paper in every book contains 10% to 30% post-consumer waste (PCW). The cover board on the outside of each book contains 100% PCW. Our goal is to do our part to help young people and the environment too!

Photo Credits: © DigitalVision, 10, 13, 17, 24, 43, 57; © iStockphoto.com/Chris Schmidt, 32, © iStockphoto.com/Elizabeth Shoemaker, 55; © 2008 Jupiterimages Corporation, 21, 41; Used under license from Shutterstock, Inc., 1, 3, 4, 6, 8, 9, 16, 18, 22, 26, 28, 30, 35, 36, 37, 45, 48, 50, 52.

Cover Photo: Used under license from Shutterstock, Inc.

CONTENTS

What is Love?

> *My bounty is as boundless as the sea,*
> *My love as deep; the more I give to thee,*
> *The more I have, for both are infinite.*
>
> —*William Shakespeare,* Romeo and Juliet

What is love? That question has been discussed over many centuries. In his play *Romeo and Juliet*, seventeenth-century English writer William Shakespeare attempts to describe love's emotional depth. In the lines above, Juliet explains the intensity of her feelings for Romeo. Stories of love and longing have been told throughout history by playwrights, as well as by songwriters, authors, and filmmakers. Tales of love and loss touch a nerve in everyone, because love is something all people identify with.

Love can be many things. It can refer to the bond you feel with your parents. It can be the connection you have with your best friend. And with romantic love, it can be the feelings you have for someone special in your life—one that involves both emotional feelings and the pull of physical attraction. Although these are different kinds of love, all involve many of the same elements.

You and Your Emotions

A part of everyone's personality, emotions are a powerful driving force in life. They are hard to define and understand. But what is known is that emotions—which include anger, fear, love, joy, jealousy, and hate—are a normal part of the human system. They are responses to situations and events that trigger bodily changes, motivating you to take some kind of action.

Some studies show that the brain relies more on emotions than on intellect in learning and in making decisions. Being able to identify and understand the emotions in yourself and in others can help you in your relationships with family, friends, and others throughout your life.

They include trust, loyalty, support, and encouragement. However, one of the most important ingredients in love is the intense feeling of caring for another person.

Having close relationships is important. They give you the chance to understand what is important to you. And they give you experience in sharing and trusting others. Learning about love means learning about yourself.

Understanding yourself and your feelings is a big part of growing up. And right now in your life, there is plenty to try to figure out. It's likely you're dealing with physical changes occurring in your body due to

"Love makes your soul crawl out from its hiding place."

–Zora Neale Hurston

Puberty can be a confusing time. Don't worry! The feelings you have are only temporary. You'll soon figure things out.

puberty. This is the stage of life when your body is developing from that of a child to an adult.

Growing up. As you go through puberty, you may feel uncomfortable with your body as certain parts are growing and changing shape. These physical changes are the result of sometimes drastic changes in your body's hormone levels. Hormones are special chemical substances that carry messages regulating the activity of cells. In girls, the most important hormones are estrogen and progesterone.

As the amounts of hormones in your body change, you can feel emotional upheavals and experience extreme mood swings. As a result, the way you relate to others can be bumpy at times. Feelings of longing and romantic

Puberty refers to the time when a young person's body is developing and changing as she becomes an adult. In girls, puberty usually starts between ages eight and thirteen.

Love

attraction to others become stronger during puberty, too. These feelings can be physical, affecting sexual behavior and desire, and emotional, involving a longing for closeness and for a feeling of being connected to someone else.

People grow physically and emotionally at different rates. One girl may begin the changes of puberty at age eight, while another might be thirteen years old. And boys typically begin puberty even later. As a result, you may find you have suddenly grown several inches, and now tower over many of the boys you know. Some of them may be interested in having a romantic relationship, while others won't be interested at all.

Falling in love. Right now, you may be thinking about what love means to you and what you would want in a

Science Says....

When a person has strong feelings toward someone else, studies show, the brain releases increased amounts of certain brain chemicals, or neurotransmitters. One of these neurotransmitters is dopamine, which causes a person to feel good.

Exposure to exciting, new things can trigger the release of dopamine, too. So if your first date includes some risky rides at an amusement park, it's likely you'll want to have a second date with that person. That's because the release of dopamine resulting from the excitement of a wild rollercoaster ride can stimulate feelings of attraction between the two of you.[1]

Science of Attraction

In his studies of what happens when people fall in love, psychologist Arthur Arun found that attraction between two people increases with the simple act of staring into each other's eyes. Researchers set up situations in which complete strangers were asked to reveal personal details about themselves to each other for an hour and a half. Then they were told to stare into each other's eyes for four minutes. Afterward, these complete strangers admitted to having strong feelings of attraction for one another. Two actually eventually married.[2]

Making eye contact when speaking to someone is key to establishing a strong connection.

Symbols of Love

Cupid, the Roman god of love: Represented as a winged boy carrying a bow and arrow, Cupid makes people fall in love by shooting an arrow through the heart.

Heart: A heart symbol is often used to replace the word *love*.

Rose: Red roses symbolize love and passion.

romantic relationship. Or maybe you are interested in someone else but haven't shared your feelings with that person. Or perhaps you are in a serious relationship. All of these situations are giving you the opportunity to grow emotionally and develop the knowledge and skills to maintain healthy relationships.

An emotional rollercoaster ride. In the course of learning about the very complicated world of romantic love, you will most likely experience a wide range of feelings. You may feel the longing for a special connection, the joys of first love, the anger of conflict, and the sorrow of breaking up. At times it may feel like your emotions are one big rollercoaster ride. If you are feeling overwhelmed by your changing moods, you may find it helpful to share your feelings with trusted friends. After all, they are probably going through the same thing, too. You may also find that your parents have some helpful insights.

As you share time with another person, you can have the opportunity to gain an understanding of yourself and your values. Remember, the ways you choose to deal with others in relationships—for example, how you treat them and expect them to treat you—will establish the person you will be as an adult.

Flattened by a Crush

Yesterday Mia saw Luke in the hallway. When he said hello, her stomach did a flip-flop. For the rest of the day she felt a warm glow inside. This morning Luke was standing by Mia's locker when she walked up. And again, her stomach flipped over. She felt herself blushing and her palms got sweaty.

Having a crush can be exciting, but it can also be intense and weigh heavily on your emotions—that's why it's called a crush. Crushes are an important part of developing relationships. When you have a crush on someone, you are discovering just what it is that you like in a person. At the same time, you are learning how to deal with the strong emotions brought on by a crush. If your crush feels the same way about you, you can feel great and on top of the world. But if he doesn't feel the same way, you may feel ignored, sad, and rejected.

It is possible to have a crush on someone you don't know at

When you are near your crush, you may find yourself blushing or feeling nervous and jittery.

An **infatuation** is a brief feeling of intense passion or admiration for someone. A **crush** is an intense infatuation with someone.

all but feel strongly attracted to. You can also develop a crush on someone you've known since grade school.

When you like someone you've known a long time. You may have been hanging out with your friend Travis since first grade. But one day, Travis seems different to you. You find yourself wondering if he's interested in you in the same way you are. You have two choices: you can keep your secret crush to yourself or you can tell him.

Before telling a friend you want to be something more than "just friends," think first about the possibility of losing his friendship. Your admission could make him uncomfortable if he doesn't feel the same way. And that can be hard for you. Be prepared for rejection. If he backs off, at least you'll know where you stand.

Even if he does feel the same way, if your romantic relationship doesn't work out in the long run, it will be hard to go back to the friendship level. (Although many teens do remain good

Crushes can be confusing, but when you have a crush on someone you are learning about yourself and the kind of person you feel attracted to. You may find you have a crush on a boy or another girl. Such feelings are okay and normal. However, if you feel confused or worried about your feelings, you should talk to a trusted adult such as a parent or other family member, your doctor, or a school counselor.

Science Says....

Several neurotransmitters play a role when people first fall in love. Extra amounts of one neurotransmitter, called dopamine, produce a blissful feeling. The increased amount of another brain chemical, norepinephrine, causes excitement, a racing heart, sweaty palms, and flushed skin. Both of these neurotransmitters can produce extreme feelings of happiness, as well as feelings of energy and focused attention. But increased amounts of dopamine and norepinephrine also cause sleeplessness and a loss of appetite.

At the same time, researchers say, people in love have lower than normal levels of another neurotransmitter known as serotonin. Decreased amounts of serotonin are associated with anxiety—a feeling of nervousness about future events. Reduced levels of serotonin have also been linked with depression—a feeling of extreme sadness and hopelessness. So in a way, falling in love can make you anxious and depressed and, some would say, feeling a little bit crazy.[1]

friends after breakups.) Before you say anything, you have to decide if you really like him enough to take that chance of losing him as a friend. On the other hand, if you don't tell your crush how you feel, you will not have the chance to find out if the he has similar feelings for you.

When you like someone you barely know. Sometimes you may find yourself interested in someone you really don't know at all. Maybe it is the new boy sitting next to

you in English class or the friend of your older brother who has been hanging out a lot at your home lately. Again, you have two choices: keep your feelings to yourself or let your crush know you are interested. It can be hard telling someone you'd like to know them better, especially if you are not sure what your crush is thinking.

One way to find out is to show him you're interested. You don't need to come right out and tell a person you like him.

If you share common interests or sports, like running on the track team at school, you will have more chances to get to know each other.

"Love is friendship set on fire."

-Jeremy Taylor

You can pass the word along through body language—that is, the way you communicate without speaking. For example, as you talk, look directly into his eyes. Pay close attention when he talks, and be sure to smile. Your body language will show him you're interested in getting to know him better.

How to Let Someone Know You're Interested

- Say hi when you see him in the hall.

- Ask for his opinions.

- Compliment him on what he's wearing.

- Ask about schoolwork: "What do you think about that last test?"

- Comment on recent school activities: "What did you think about last night's game?"

- Find common interests: music? reading? sports?

- Ask questions about the latest movies or popular TV shows.

- Look him in the eyes while you're talking.

- Make jokes ... and smile.

Strike up a conversation. There are lots of things you could talk about: the book you had to read for English class, the lab experiment you both just worked on in science class, or the last school football game. Talk about things that interest you and show curiosity about his interests. Your conversation will help you see the things you have in common.

Ask questions that require more than a yes or no answer. You might want to think ahead of time of some good "conversation starters" or "continuers" so you won't feel at a loss if there is a long pause in your conversation. As the conversation flows, you may find you share a lot in common at least as friends. And you'll find that the more practice you have in talking to guys, the easier it will be.

Make it clear you're not just flirting. Flirting refers to showing an interest without any intention of serious commitment. You really do want to learn more about him.

If you decide to tell. Many teens have a hard time telling another person they are interested in being more than "just friends." So they may ask a friend to find out if the feeling is mutual.

A better idea is to keep the situation between the two of you. This kind of communication should be kept private. If you want to know if your crush is interested in you, don't bring up the

Flirting

According to one study, people say they get the idea that someone is attracted to them:

55% through body language

38% the tone and speed of the voice

7% through what is said[2]

conversation in front of friends in the lunchroom or in class. Since you don't know what the answer is going to be, you don't need to embarrass yourself or your crush if the feelings aren't mutual.

And you don't need to come out with the direct statement, "I like you." Just extend an invitation to do something together. You could ask him to eat lunch with you that day in the lunchroom or to study together for the upcoming math test. If he's interested in you, he'll take you up on one of those offers.

If he says no. It happens. Maybe he's shy. Maybe he is simply not ready to have a romantic relationship—with anyone. Or maybe he's simply not attracted to you. To avoid the latter situation, before you say anything, do your best to read signals he may be giving out. If his body language is telling you that he's interested, let him know you're interested, too.

If you get turned down by your crush, let it go. The worst thing you can do is pester or annoy him. Respect his decision and leave him alone.

If you misread his signals and the answer to your invitation is a definite no, try to act relaxed. Give a smile, say "Okay," and go find something else to do. Meet up with a good friend for a little sympathy or head for the library to work on that term paper. If you feel like crying, find a private place to let the emotions flow.

Tell yourself that it is okay. When you take chances in relationships, disappointments can happen. It hurts when you have been rejected. But accept it, leave him alone, and try to move on.

Romantic relationships can bring on a multitude of emotions—fear that he may not like you and sadness if the answer is no. You can feel uncomfortable, scared and nervous. But maybe your crush is feeling the same way. You'll never know unless you ask. The possibility of a good outcome—that you'll hear yes and have the chance to get to know your crush better—can be worth the risks of rejection.

If you are rejected by your crush, don't let your disappointment drag you down. Distract yourself by working on your term paper or catching up on some reading.

"The best and most beautiful things in the world cannot be seen or even touched—they must be felt with the heart."

–Helen Keller

Getting to Know You

Some of Jasmine's friends were going over to Joe's house to watch some movies—everyone invited was bringing something to eat, along with a favorite scary video. Jasmine was looking forward to seeing Michael there. He had told her he didn't really know Joe very well, but he was going because he wanted to see her.

Sometimes the best way to get to know someone better is to spend time with them when with friends. With group dates you have the chance to see how that person treats other people. At the same time, you can see how he behaves toward you.

Hanging out with your crush in a group setting is a relaxed way to get to know each other.

Getting to Know You

- Get to know a person by talking on the phone or at school before you go out for the first time.

- Go out with a group of friends to a public place the first few times you go out.

- Plan fun activities like going to the movies or the mall, on a picnic, or for a walk.

- Tell the other person what you feel okay doing. Also, tell the person what time your parents or guardians want you to be home.

- Tell your parents or guardians and at least one friend who you are going out with and where you are going. Also make sure they know how to reach you.[1]

You may have been hanging out with this person all along, but suddenly now find yourself attracted to him. In that case, you've already had the opportunity to see that he has a great sense of humor and that he tries to be a good friend to his buddies. If the group sometimes meets at his house, you've had the chance to see how he relates with his family—for instance, how he treats his younger brother or talks to his parents. You might decide that he is the kind of person you'd like to spend more time with.

When you get together with someone you like and who likes you, you may prefer seeing him along with the rest of your friends. A group date can be a less intense way to go out.

If you invite your crush to attend the party celebrating the end of your field hockey season, you can feel good knowing that he wanted to be your date for the event. But you don't need to worry about keeping the conversation going all the time because lots of other people will be around.

What is the right age to start dating? For many girls, their parents usually set the rules for when it is okay to date. Some young people start as young as twelve or thirteen; others may not start until they are sixteen or seventeen or even older.

Several factors—your age, the age of the person you want to date, or your family's culture or religious beliefs—can affect whether your parents think you should date. They may also be concerned about what dating means to you: Is it your close friendship with the classmate you consider your "steady," but see only at school? Or is it someone you actually go out with—to dances, movies, and school events?

Talk to your parents. When you really like someone, try to share your feelings with your parents. Even if you may find it difficult, you'll know that they will appreciate your effort to keep communication open with them. And, if you are feeling confused over how you feel about someone else, you may find that talking about the

"To the world, you're just one person, but to one person you can mean the world."

–Anonymous

situation with your mother or father may help you figure out your feelings.

Depending on how old you are, your parents may have to be more involved in your dates than you want them to. For example, if you live in the suburbs and don't have a car or driver's license, you may need to ask your parent or guardian to drive you places. However, most teens prefer to find alternative forms of transportation, says *Teen People*, which reported that 91 percent of surveyed teens didn't like to have a parent chauffeur them around on a date.[2] If public transportation is available, you may have the option of taking the bus or subway.

Your parents may have strong ideas about how late you should stay out when on a date. Recognize that they have the

If you don't want to ask your parents to drive you on your date, you can take the bus to your local mall. You can walk around, show each other your favorite kinds of music, and get some dinner.

Internet Safety Tips

Is it possible to get to know someone online? Keep in mind that people may not be who they say they are. Be careful when you see an instant message from someone you don't know. Your best bet is not to respond. Here are some other Internet safety tips to keep in mind:

- Never give out personal information such as your name, home address, school name, or telephone number in a chat room or on bulletin boards.

- Never write to someone who has made you feel uncomfortable or scared.

- Do not arrange to meet someone you've met online or have them visit you without checking with your parents first.

- Be careful about making friends or flirting online. Because some people lie online about who they really are, you don't really know who you're dealing with.

- If you feel threatened by someone or uncomfortable because of something online, tell an adult you trust. Report your concerns to the police.[3,4]

right to set a curfew—a time when they want you home. They want to know where you are and to have you home at a reasonable hour because they care about you. Keep in mind that they are looking out to keep you safe—they are not setting rules to cause problems for you.

Follow the rules. Whatever the case, you need to be clear about your parents' rules and restrictions. Before making specific plans for a date, be sure to have a talk with them about their expectations. If you don't agree with your parents' restrictions, tell them how their specific rules and curfew time make you feel. Ask—calmly and politely—if you can discuss these rules further.

Although your parents may be willing to listen to your side of the issue and to your suggested alternative, they do have the final say. If they insist that their curfew time doesn't change, you need to accept the situation and follow their rules. Don't stay out late on a date and make them worry about you. If you show them that you can be responsible about following their rules, they may be willing to talk about making some changes to family rules and curfews in the future.

In a survey of 1,000 thirteen- to seventeen-year-olds, 71 percent reported that they live in a household with curfews. About three-quarters of the teens agreed with the rules their parents had set.[5]

So... Um... Do You Want to Go Out?

Whenever Marcus walks into the classroom, Alexa has to look away so he can't see that she's blushing. She thinks he is the coolest guy in the school. Since they have been working together on the play presentation for English class, she thinks he has been acting especially nice to her, too. But he still hasn't asked her out on a date.

When you ask a guy out on a date, you are sending a message. Your invitation lets him know that you are looking at the possibility of establishing a relationship. Some guys are flattered when the girl asks them out. They admire her for taking the initiative and in making her interest clear. However, others aren't so comfortable with the idea of girls asking boys out on dates, and would react with an automatic no. If you're comfortable being the asker, you probably don't want to

Getting up the nerve to ask out a classmate is hard for both girls and guys.

Asking Him Out

"Would you like to go to the school football game/basketball game/dance together? "

"There's a new movie opening this weekend that I'd like to see. Would you like to see it with me?"

"I've got tickets to the <fill in the blank> concert. Would you like to go?"

go out with the guy who has problems with being asked out by a girl. It is not likely you'll have much in common.

Why go on a date? Teens give various reasons for wanting to date. Some say they figure they should be dating because everyone else in their group is dating. Others admit they want to date the person who is considered most popular in their school. Still others say they want to annoy their parents by dating a person they don't like.

However, the best reason to date someone is because you have feelings for the person and want to get to know him better. You're looking to develop a bond with someone. You want to share your thoughts and feelings with that person, to spend time with him and enjoy his company.

"If you are never scared, embarrassed or hurt, it means you never take chances."

–Julia Soul

How to act on a first date and a second and a third. . . . If you're going out for the first time on a date that will involve just the two of you, try to leave your worries at home. If you're really nervous, it can be awkward for both of you. Relax. Make a joke and laugh at yourself if you trip on the stairs or knock over the water glass at the restaurant. Keep in mind that he's probably feeling nervous, too. And remember, the idea of a date is to have a good time with someone whose company you enjoy.

Keep some of these suggestions in mind whenever you're on a date.

- If you're meeting at a location other than home, be on time. If you're meeting at your home, be ready on time.

- During the date, don't spend a lot of time talking about yourself. Ask questions, but don't overdo it by making it sound like a job interview. Listen to the answers before speaking. Treat him with respect by giving him attention.

Snowboarding can be a fun way to spend a date. If you like sports, other dates to consider might include playing tennis or rollerblading.

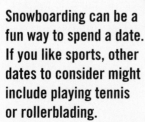

- Be sure to share information about yourself, but don't dominate the conversation.

- Be honest. Don't make up stories about yourself or people you know in order to impress him.

- Be flexible. If plans get messed up—for example, the baseball tournament you were to watch together was cancelled because of heavy rains, suggest a drier alternative, like a trip to the movies.

You'll find that you can learn a lot about another person when you're on a date. In the beginning of a relationship, both of you will probably be very self conscious and on your best

Some Inexpensive Dates

- Take a walk around the neighborhood.

- If you live in the city, ride the bus or subway around town.

- Invite a group to volunteer together in a nursing home or hospital.

- Invite everyone to your house for an ice cream sundae party or a barbeque.

- Organize a group bike ride.

- Attend school games or musical performances together.

- Go miniature golfing or bowling.

Who Pays?

If you asked him out, say to a dance at your school and he goes to a different school, you should plan to pay. After all, you're the one who initiated the date in the first place. If he's the one who asked you out, you could offer to contribute to the costs of really expensive dates, such as music concerts. Even if you believe your date will be paying, be sure to have enough money with you to help out if he misplaces his wallet!

behavior. Over time, your regular, day-to-day personalities will come out as you both become more comfortable being around each other. But what if he treats you well, but is rude to your

After a few dates, you'll begin to get to know the "real" guy. As you get to know each other, you'll begin to feel more comfortable together.

parents? Or if he is mean to the waitress at the restaurant or the cashier at the fast food place? He may have a mean streak in him that could one day be directed at you, too. Let him know when you don't like his behavior. If he doesn't seem to care, you may want to think about making this your last date together.

If you don't feel comfortable during the date and want to leave early, be prepared. Have a cell phone with you in case you need to call for a ride. It can also be useful to have a phone if you feel like you need to remove yourself from an unsafe situation.

However, if things are working out okay, enjoy yourself. Learning about another person who attracts you can be fun. Just remember to be honest with yourself about why you are hanging out with this person and what you would like to relationship to be.

Turning Down Someone You Don't Want to Date

Don't lead a guy on because you're flattered by the attention. If you are not interested, be honest and direct, but kind. A statement like, "I'm sorry, but I really don't want to go out with you," lets the person know where he stands. Don't make up stories about having something else to do that day because he will be likely to try again and ask another time. If he is persistent, you need to repeat yourself until it is clear: "I said no and you should respect that." Keep his invitation private. The rest of the world doesn't have to know.

Good Together

You two have had a few dates. After school, you ride home together on the bus. You talk on the phone or chat over the Internet every night. You eat lunch together in the cafeteria. You hang out together as much as you can. You hold hands wherever you go.

Is it love? Don't let your friends tell you what you're feeling or make you think you have to be in love. What your relationship means depends on what you and your boyfriend think. If you are wondering whether you're really in love, give

Real love takes time to blossom and grow. Take your time getting to know your boyfriend.

Is This Love? Some Questions to Consider

- Am I willing to wait for this person if he is not ready to have a more physical relationship?

- Am I willing to give up some of my goals and dreams to allow his dreams to come true?

- Do I respect and admire this person?

- Would I feel the same way about this person if he got sick?

- When we disagree, does the argument change the way I feel about him?

If you answered no to any of the above questions, your feelings of love might not be strong enough to maintain a long-lasting relationship.

yourself some time. Think about what love means to you. Meanwhile, recognize that you can continue to enjoy your relationship and your strong feelings for another person without having to label it as "love." After all, it is also possible that your feelings will change at some point, and you will end your relationship.

During the first stages of dating, what you're feeling is likely to be more of an infatuation than love, says professor Cynthia Hazan. She estimates that the infatuation stage in a romantic relationship can last anywhere from eighteen to thirty months.

If the relationship remains strong, at some point around that time, she says, your idealized views of each other will change and form into an even stronger bond of love.[1]

Even during the so-called infatuation stage, you will want to keep the good feelings about your relationship strong. All healthy relationships rest on a few very fundamental principles.

Trust. To trust someone is to firmly believe that the person will be reliable—he will be there for you when you need him because he wants be there. It typically means you can count on him not to flirt with other girls or say things

If you are always second guessing the truthfulness of what your boyfriend is saying, chances are the relationship is not going to last.

about you that might hurt you. If the trust between the two of you is shaky, something is wrong. If you feel you can't trust your boyfriend, the relationship isn't very strong.

Honesty. This element of a good relationship is very similar to trust. When you trust a person, you believe in his or her honesty. That person will be truthful and sincere with you. And you will behave the same way.

In your relationship, you need to be honest about who you are—don't pretend to be someone you're not. For instance, don't pretend to be really interested in things he likes if you really aren't. On the other hand, though, you should try to be open to learning new things, too.

Be honest about what you do and don't know. Similarly, don't play games and say things that aren't true. If you don't want to go to the baseball game with him, say so. Don't make up a story about having to go to your grandmother's birthday party that afternoon, when the party is really next weekend. If you get caught in a lie, what will he think of you? And for that matter, how good will you feel about yourself?

How Committed Are You?

If you're not sure about your feelings in a relationship, give yourself time. You may find it helpful to take a break from each other. Use the time you spend apart to think about your feelings. Do you miss the person? Or do you have feelings of being attracted to others? If you are finding that you are more interested in meeting new people, you may not be ready to settle into a committed relationship.

"The first duty of love is to listen."

–Paul Tillich

Good communication.

A major key to any relationship is communication. When one or both of you get mad, it's important that you talk to each other. Giving someone the silent treatment when you're angry doesn't do anything to fix the problem. If you want to resolve a conflict, you need to discuss the problem and come up with solutions.

Be direct about what has upset you or made you unhappy. Was it something he said or did last week? If so, tell him. "I was upset that you missed watching my playoff game. You said you'd be there, and I wanted to see you cheering me on at the sidelines." Do your best to stay calm so you can clearly explain your side of the issue. But if you lose your cool, let him know it is because the situation means a lot to you and it is hard for you to talk calmly about it.

Good communication is more than talking, though. You also need to listen. Give him time to state things from his point of view. If he doesn't seem to want to talk, let him know how important it is to you that you understand where he's coming from. Make it clear that you have a problem. If he doesn't want to help solve it, then it may mean things between you are not very good.

Respect.

To respect someone means to pay attention and give value to the feelings, rights, and wishes of the other person. In other words, it means treating the other person as you would like to be treated yourself.

When you are bothered about something, you need to state your point of view in a way that is respectful of the other

person. Avoid being aggressive in your arguments. That is, don't say whatever comes to mind, without thinking and without respect for the other person. Put-downs, hurtful words, and name-calling are all aggressive forms of communication. These kinds of words cause hard feelings and often lead to more hostility. If you want to solve problems, be assertive, not aggressive.

Communication Blockers

Be aware that the way you respond to the person you have a conflict with may keep you from understanding the problem. Certain behaviors that prevent your ability to hear what the other person is saying are called "communication blockers." They include:

Interrupting. If you keep butting in when the other person is trying to talk, how can you hear what he has to say?

Challenging, accusing, or contradicting. By arguing, you are forcing the other person to be defensive. Instead of resolving the fight you may be starting a new one.

Criticizing, name-calling, or putting-down. Sarcastic and negative comments can bring any conversation to an end—well before any conflicts are resolved.

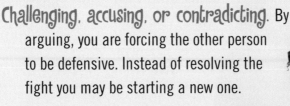

A Balancing Act

Your friends want to celebrate Madison's birthday this weekend with a movie, your family has planned a Saturday afternoon visit to Aunt Selma, and you've told your boyfriend you'll go to his dad's birthday party that night. Will there be time to fit in the special tryouts for chorus that you told your teacher you were planning to attend?

The feeling of wanting to spend every waking moment with the special person in your life can be so strong that it interferes with your other relationships. Studies have shown that girls in particular can become so involved with their romance that they push away friends and family.[1] Although you may want to spend all of your time with your significant other, it is important not to overlook the relationships with the other people in your life.

Making time for friends. No matter how much your love interest means to you, don't leave your friends behind in the dust. Be sure to set aside time for activities with just your girlfriends. And treat them with respect—don't change your plans to go out with them when your boyfriend asks you to do something else at the last minute.

Make time to do things with your friends. Don't forget about them just because you have a boyfriend.

It is not healthy for a relationship if the two of you spend every moment with each other. One teen described an intense relationship with her boyfriend: "It got to the point where I didn't want to do anything or go anywhere without him," she explained. "I hardly cared about being with my friends anymore, and I couldn't understand why he would want to be with his."[2]

Unfortunately, this behavior hurt the relationship. The girl explained, "We started to grow apart because of this, which made me even more obsessed with spending time with him. We would pick fights with each other for reasons I couldn't remember the next day."[3] The two eventually broke up.

In some cases, your friends may not like your boyfriend. If they are always putting him down in front of you, you may begin to doubt yourself and your judgment. Don't let them decide who you should be dating. Be honest with yourself. If you have strong feelings for the guy, just acknowledge their point of view—and ask them to stop: "I know you don't like him, but I do. I don't need to hear any more nasty comments." However, if your friends have legitimate reasons to be concerned about whether you should be dating your boyfriend, listen with an open mind to what they have to say. They may be worried about you.

Balancing your relationship with your family. Sometimes a new romantic relationship can cause

The Surveys Say...

In a poll taken by *Teen People* magazine, teens said that . . .

. . . 34% were currently in a relationship.

. . . 21% had never dated anyone.

. . . 45% thought that having a boyfriend or girlfriend was not important.

. . . 39% had sent a crush an anonymous love note.

. . . 48% had received a letter or gift from a secret admirer.

. . . 28% would rather go out with their best friends than with a date.[4]

issues between parents and daughters. This can be especially true if the girl becomes so involved with her boyfriend that she no longer makes time to be with the family.

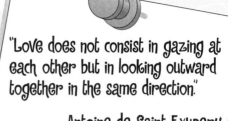

"Love does not consist in gazing at each other but in looking outward together in the same direction."

–Antoine de Saint-Exupery

You can avoid these issues if you keep your parents in the loop. Give details about what you're doing. Get permission from them before you say yes to plans with your boyfriend, especially if you need your mother or father to help with transportation. Rather than argue with your parents about the amount of time you're spending with your boyfriend, think up solutions so you can have it both ways. For example, suggest an outing to the beach, a hike at the state park, or a bike ride—something that you can do with your family but also invite the boyfriend along, too.

When parents have concerns. Some parents don't allow their daughters to date until they reach a certain age. Others may forbid a daughter from dating a boy who is a few years older. Still others may have objections to her dating someone of a different race or religion. Or they may have accepted the relationship at the beginning but have come to believe that the boyfriend is not treating their daughter very well.

What do you do when you want to date someone and your parents say no? Keep in mind that the traits of honesty and communication are just as important in your relationship with your parents as they are in a romantic relationship. The worst thing you can do is ignore your folks and sneak around behind their back. You need to demonstrate to your parents that you

Avoiding and Handling Conflicts with Parents

- Discuss the rules ahead of time so you understand your parents' expectations.

- Follow the rules. If your plans mean you'll be late for curfew, let them know and ask if you can have an exemption to the rule.

- Pick your battles. Avoid fights over every little thing. If you are going to argue, make sure you focus on the issues that are important to you.

- Don't lose your temper. Try to remain calm when your parents say no about something.

- Talk, don't yell. Listen to what your parents have to say.

- Watch your body language. Don't roll your eyes or wear a frown on your face.

- Calmly, but firmly, explain your side of the issue.

- Ask your parents to give you the same respect that they want from you.

- Accept their decision gracefully, even if it is not the response you wanted.

are honest by abiding by their wishes. But you can ask them if they will show you the same respect by talking with you about why they are not comfortable about letting you decide who you wish to date.

Although it may feel as if your parents are setting unfair rules to upset you, realize that they are only looking out for your best interests. If you disagree with them, talk to them.

Ask your parents if you could sit down and have a talk so you can give your side of the issue. Have a conversation—not a shouting match. By keeping your temper, you are showing them you are a mature person. In time, you may be able to bring them around so they agree with your wishes. However, if that does not occur, it is important that you respect their wishes and maintain the trust they have in you.

"Be a good listener. Your ears will never get you in trouble."

—Frank Tyger

Feeling Pressures, Making Choices

> *Emily has a problem. Her boyfriend, Mark, wants her to go to Nate's party this weekend. But Ali just told her that Nate's parents won't be there. And some kids are talking about bringing some beer. Emily has told Mark that she doesn't feel comfortable about going to Nate's party. She knows her parents would be furious with her if they found out. But Mark keeps insisting that it's okay—that she doesn't need to let her parents know. He says she should just say she's at Ali's house for a sleepover.*

The "respect" part of a healthy relationship means you should never feel pressured to do something you don't want to do. If you feel uncomfortable about something, you have the right to say so.

But it can be hard when you feel pressure from a boyfriend or other friends to go along with whatever the crowd is doing—and you don't want to. This is especially true when it comes to making important decisions about smoking or drinking alcohol. Peer pressure—the influence of kids your own age—can be hard to oppose, especially if you think your boyfriend or your friends won't like you anymore if you don't do what they're doing.

Peer pressure. When individuals become part of a group, they can often stop thinking for themselves. Instead, they let the group determine what they will do or not do. Just remember, you'll feel better about yourself in the long run if

Having more freedom includes the responsibility to make the right decision—no matter what your friends are doing.

you stay true to yourself and what you believe in. If you cross the line, and do something that makes you uncomfortable, you'll feel terrible afterward. Trust your instincts. If you think something is wrong, then it probably is.

Remember, your real friends will recognize you are doing what you think is right. They will respect your decisions. Even people who tease or criticize you may secretly admire your ability to choose the thing that's right for you!

The right to say no. The same holds true for a boyfriend. If he respects you, he'll respect your values and choices. He won't pressure you to do something you don't want to do, including using illegal drugs or drinking alcohol, or anything else you feel uncomfortable about. He will recognize that

Tips for a Healthy Relationship

Remember that the relationship is between the two of you. Don't tell others things that he would want to keep private.

Don't be overly possessive: Let him spend time with his buddies. It's healthy for couples to do things apart from each other.

Stay true to yourself. Don't change the way you dress, how you wear your hair, or your behavior because he's said so. Don't pretend to like his music, hobbies, or interests if you really don't.

Keep your independence. Don't let him define who you are or depend on him for everything.

you have the right to say no without being teased, insulted—or even worse—threatened.

These rights also hold true in any decisions you and your boyfriend make in your physical relationship. Pressures to have a sexual relationship can be especially strong in today's society, in which television, books, magazines, movies, and music often focus on sex. One 2005 study reported that among the top 20 most watched shows by teens, 70 percent included sexual content and 45 percent included sexual behavior.[1] Few of these shows included mention of accompanying risks such as sexually transmitted diseases (STDs) and pregnancy. For the most part, they played down the importance of sexual responsibility.[2]

Dating expectations. Making decisions about how you want to show physical affection begins with your first date. If you don't feel comfortable giving a "goodnight kiss," you have the right to say so. And you have the right to choose not to have sex—to practice abstinence—if that is what seems right for you.

Any kind of sexual activity should be treated very seriously. Being sexually active can lead to all kinds of serious consequences—from pregnancy to sexually transmitted diseases to emotional problems. Condoms are a form of contraception that can help prevent pregnancy as well as some STDs; however, they are not 100 percent effective. Be careful, and remember that the safest sex is abstinence—not having sex at all. If you need more information, you may want to speak to your parents, a health teacher or guidance counselor, a doctor, or other trusted adult.

Remember, you have the right to say no if there is something you don't feel comfortable about.

Before you find yourself in a situation where you have to make a sudden decision, give the consequences of a physical relationship some serious thought. It is important to think about how your actions can affect other people, including your parents, particularly if a sexually transmitted disease or unwanted pregnancy occurs. Know ahead of time how you want to behave. Then be sure to make sure your boyfriend understands how you feel.

In a good relationship, your boyfriend will understand and accept your values and beliefs. If you are feeling pressured to have a physical relationship to "prove your love," it's time to think again about your entire relationship. Do you really want to be with someone who has no problem pushing you to do things you don't want to do? If he is not respecting your wishes, he doesn't really value you.

Abusive relationships. Because they are often new to romantic relationships, many teens become involved in unhealthy or abusive relationships without realizing it. An extremely jealous boyfriend may be controlling, or emotionally abusive. He may demand that his girlfriend not speak to any other boys, or he may call her frequently to find out what she is doing and who she is with. Although the girl may feel flattered at first by her boyfriend's attention, she can soon become overwhelmed and frightened by his jealousy and possessiveness.

The jealous boyfriend can also be verbally or physically abusive. When the girl has had enough and tries to break up with him, he typically claims to be sorry and begs for another chance, often saying, "It won't happen again." Unfortunately, without counseling, the abusive boyfriend will most likely continue to repeat his bad behavior.

Common Sexually Transmitted Diseases (STDs)

It is possible to contract many of these diseases and not have any symptoms. When not detected and treated, STDs can cause serious health problems and even death.

AIDS: A viral disease that attacks and wears down the immune system. Acquired immune deficiency syndrome (AIDS) is caused by the human immunodeficiency virus (HIV).

Chlamydia: An infection caused by the bacterium *Chlamydia trachomatis*.

Genital herpes: A viral infection caused by the herpes simplex virus (HSV) that can cause blisters or sores.

Gonorrhea: An infection caused by the bacterium *Neisseria gonorrhoeae*.

Human papillomavirus (HPV): A virus that can cause cancer of the cervix (the opening to the uterus); a vaccine is available to prevent the disease.

Syphilis: An infection caused by the bacterium *Treponema pallidum*.

Trichomoniasis: An infection caused by the parasite *Trichomonas vaginalis*.

A CDC study estimates that one in four young women between the ages of fourteen and nineteen in the United States is infected with at least one of the four most common sexually transmitted diseases—chlamydia, HPV, HSV, and trichomoniasis.[3]

A 2005 study commissioned by Liz Claiborne Inc. found that more than half (57 percent) of teens ages thirteen through eighteen knew friends or peers who have been physically, sexually, or verbally abused.[4]

Girls in destructive relationships of this sort typically become afraid to express their own opinions. They begin to doubt themselves and their abilities. As a result, they often remain trapped in the relationship, feeling helpless and powerless to do anything about it.

According to most experts, a girl in this kind of situation is in danger of getting seriously hurt. Encourage her to talk to a parent or other adult friend, contact a local battered women's shelter, or call the domestic violence or youth crisis telephone hotline number listed on page 61. If she doesn't take action, tell her you will.

Love should make you feel happy and secure—not anxious and afraid.

Signs of an Unhealthy Relationship

You are in an unhealthy and abusive relationship when the person you are going out with:

- Is jealous or possessive of you.

- Bosses you around, makes all the decisions, and tells you what to do.

- Tells you what to wear, who to talk to, and where you can go.

- Calls to check up on you all the time.

- Makes you feel scared of how he will react to things.

- Insults you or tries to embarrass you in front of other people.

- Swears at you or uses mean language.

- Uses drugs and alcohol and tries to pressure you into doing the same thing.

- Pressures you to have sex or to do something sexual that you don't want to do.

- Is violent to other people, gets in fights a lot, and loses his temper a lot.

- Has physically hurt you.

- Blames you for his problems, and tells you that it is your fault that he hurt you.[5]

Breaking Up and Starting Over

You just celebrated your first anniversary together. But lately you've been bothered by certain things. Does he always have to comb his hair every time he passes a mirror? And that habit of cracking his knuckles is really getting on your nerves. But the worst thing is how much he's been flirting with other girls, even after you told him it bothers you.

he magic is gone. Or something has happened so things between you don't feel right anymore. Whatever the case, you have two options: keep trying to make the relationship work or decide to put an end to it.

Maybe you think your boyfriend is not treating you well because he's flirting with other girls. Or he's taking you for granted, assuming you'll be available whenever he calls. You'd still like to stay together, but something has got to change. If

Relationships can end because one or both of you have changed.

How Long Does It Last?

A 2000 survey asked kids ages twelve through nineteen about how long their last relationship lasted.

1 day	1%
A few days	4%
1-3 weeks	11%
1-2 months	16%
3-6 months	19%
7 months to 1 year	10%
More than 1 year	14%
Never had a romance	22%[1]

you tell him that and he doesn't apologize, it may be that he's already been thinking that it's time to go your separate ways. On the other hand, he may promise to treat you better, but not follow through. In that case, he's not treating you with respect—and you deserve better than that.

Before you give up on the relationship, try to make sure you understand where your boyfriend is coming from. It may be that he has a hard time sharing his feelings—with anyone. Lots of guys have a hard time expressing their emotions, but they feel just as strongly about their romances as girls do, says professor of sociology Peggy Giordano. In her study involving seventh, ninth, and

"'Tis better to have loved and lost than never to have loved at all."

–Alfred Lord Tennyson

eleventh graders, she found that boys were just as emotionally committed to their romantic relationships as girls were.[2]

If you think the time has come for your relationship to end, keep in mind it will hurt your boyfriend as much as it does you. On the other hand, don't put off a breakup because you feel guilty that you might hurt your steady. If you really believe it is time to break up, he needs to know.

When you decide to break up. If you haven't been dating for too long—maybe you've had only two or three dates—then talking about a formal breakup is not really necessary. Just don't invite him to do anything else with you. If he asks you out on another date, simply say, "No, I'd rather not."

Breaking up is never easy. It's a delicate subject and should be handled that way.

When You Want to Break Up

1. Don't ignore him and hope he gets the message.
2. Don't tell him in a phone call.
3. Don't give him the news in a text message.
4. Don't inform him in an e-mail or instant message.
5. Don't have one of your friends deliver the news.

However, if you and your boyfriend have been dating seriously, you owe it to each other to have a talk.

The act of breaking up makes most people feel awkward and uncomfortable. So, it can be tempting to simply say nothing at all, and just start avoiding the other person. Or you might have your girlfriend deliver the bad news to your boyfriend in a note, then tell all your friends and hope he gets the message. That is a lousy way to treat someone, especially the person you once had strong feelings for.

Choose the right place and time to have a talk. The ideal place would be a private location where you're not likely to be interrupted—not in the school lunchroom or at a party. Choose a place where you can leave after you're done talking.

Figure out what you want to say beforehand. Be direct, and say the obvious: "I don't want to go out anymore." Be prepared to give reasons why you want to end the relationship and to answer any questions. Unless you are really not sure that you

want a clean break, try not to get involved in any arguments or negotiation. Let him know you won't change your mind.

When it's not your idea. If the breakup is his idea, and it comes out of the blue, you will probably be feeling overwhelmed by your emotions. It's perfectly normal to cry and feel sad and even depressed when a relationship has ended. It hurts. You have suffered a loss. The sad feelings resulting from a breakup can make you feel physically sick, lose your appetite, and have trouble thinking about other things in your life.

Don't blame yourself for what happened, thinking if you were a different person or had behaved differently you'd still be together. What's important is to realize that when somebody falls out of love with you, it's not your fault. What is more likely is that one or both of you have grown and changed— and so have your feelings. Don't waste your energy imagining ways to get him back. Acknowledge that the relationship is over and that it is time to move on.

Feelings of depression. It is normal to feel sad about a breakup. However, sometimes the deep sense of loss and sad feelings may last a long time. When they are accompanied by a lack of interest in life, persistant sad feelings can lead to a mental disorder known as clinical depression. This is especially true in teens who have strained relationships with parents or who engage in drug and alcohol use. Some experts say 15 percent to 20 percent of teens—especially younger teens—will have diagnosable depression at some time during adolescence.[3]

Other things besides breakups can trigger clinical depression. Stressful life events such as parental divorce or a death in the family can also lead to the disorder. But it is a serious mental

Some of the Symptoms of Clinical Depression

- A loss of interest in activities previously enjoyed
- Withdrawing from friends and family
- Difficulty concentrating and making decisions
- Feelings of worthlessness or guilt
- Fatigue or loss of energy
- Appetite or weight changes
- Headaches, stomachaches, other body pains
- Suicidal thoughts

disorder that can lead to suicide. That's why it's important that the person suffering from clinical depression receive medical attention as soon as possible. With counseling or a combination of drug therapy and counseling, the disorder is treatable.

Helping a Friend

If you are worried about a friend who seems clinically depressed or possibly suicidal (giving away possessions, avoiding friends, talking about or obsessed with death), you need to get help for that person. Talk to a trusted adult or call the suicide prevention hotline listed on page 61.

Coping with Feelings of Loss

Take care of yourself physically. Get enough sleep, eat healthy foods, and exercise regularly.

Don't focus your thoughts on what happened. Instead, try to think about other possibilities in your life. Set new goals for yourself and your future.

Get busy with something else. Listen to music, watch a movie, play an instrument, or go for a run. Join a new club or after-school activity.

Get together with friends. If you do want to talk to someone about what has happened, choose a friend you can trust to keep your private thoughts private.

Don't spread nasty rumors about your ex. Trying to "get even" won't accomplish anything except make you look bad.

Take time for yourself to get over your breakup. Don't rush into any new relationships.

Moving on and starting over. For most people, the breakup of a relationship results in sad feelings that fade with time. It's okay to feel sad for a while. In fact, it can take up to several months to get over a breakup. Just keep telling yourself, eventually everything will be okay.

Replace negative thoughts—that the breakup happened because there is something wrong with you—with positive ones. Tell yourself that you are a great person with lots of good qualities. Maybe your friends have told you that you're easy to

Be there for your friends, and they'll be there for you in times of need.

talk to or that you have a great sense of humor. They know you have much to offer in a relationship and sometime in the future someone else out there will see it, too.

Continue to make efforts to develop new friendships. Who knows, you may find that one of those new relationships you've made will blossom into a new romantic one. And you will now have the benefit of bringing experience from your past relationship to a new one.

As you share time with a new person, you can look back on how your behavior affected a previous romantic relationship. And you can apply what you learned so you can develop an even better relationship than you had before. With each new relationship, you will learn more about what it means to love and be loved.

Chapter 1. What Is Love?

1. Lauren Slater, "Love," *National Geographic*, February 2006, p. 49.

2. "Science & Nature: Hot Topics: The Science of Flirting," *BBC*, November 18, 2004, <http://www.bbc.co.uk/science/hottopics/love/flirting.shtml> (April 27, 2008).

Chapter 2. Flattened by a Crush

1. "Science & Nature: Hot Topics: The Science of Love: Key Points," *BBC*, November 18, 2004, <http://www.bbc.co.uk/science/hottopics/love/index.shtml> (April 27, 2008).

2. "Science & Nature: Hot Topics: The Science of Flirting," *BBC*, November 18, 2004, <http://www.bbc.co.uk/science/hot-topics/love/flirting.shtml> (April 27, 2008).

Chapter 3. Getting to Know You

1. "Relationships: Dating," *girlshealth.gov*, n.d., <http://www.4girls.gov/relationships/dating.htm> (April 27, 2008).

2. "Trend Poll," *Teen People*, March 2002.

3. Adapted from "Safety Tips: Internet Safety," *Federal Bureau of Investigation*, n.d., <http://www.fbi.gov/kids/k5th/safety2.htm> (April 27, 2008).

4. Adapted from "Facts for Consumers: Social Networking Sites: Safety Tips for Tweens and Teens," *Federal Trade Commission*, May 2006, <http://www.ftc.gov/bcp/edu/pubs/consumer/tech/tec14.shtm> (April 27, 2008).

5. "Setting Teen Curfews," *iVillage*, n.d., <http://www.parenting.ivillage.com/teen/tsocial/0,,5jxs,00.html> (April 27, 2008).

Chapter 5. Good Together

1. Kathleen Kelleher, "Birds & Bees: Sure, True Love Sounds Ideal, but What Does It Actually Mean?" *Los Angeles Times*, May 15, 2000, p. 2.

Chapter 6. A Balancing Act

1. Amy Dickinson, "Puppy Love's Bite," *Time*, April 16, 2001, p. 82.

2. Dorothy [no last name], "Letting Go," *Teen Ink*, February 2006, p. 37.

3. Ibid.

4. "Trend Poll," *Teen People*, March 2002.

Chapter 7. Feeling Pressures, Making Choices

1. "Number of Sexual Scenes on TV Nearly Double Since 1998," *Henry J. Kaiser Family Foundation*, November 9, 2005, <http://www.kff.org/entmedia/entmedia110905nr.cfm> (April 27, 2008).

2. Lisa de Moraes, "Television More Oversexed Than Ever, Study Finds," *The Washington Post*, November 10, 2005, p. C01.

3. "Nationally Representative CDC Study Finds 1 in 4 Teenage Girls Has a Sexually Transmitted Disease," *Centers for Disease Control and Prevention*, March 11, 2008, <http://www.cdc.gov/STDConference/2008/media/release-11march2008.htm> (April 27, 2008).

4. "Liz Claiborne Inc. Omnibuzz Topline Findings: Teen Relationship Abuse Research," *Hotsheet: Teenage Research Unlimited*, February 2005, <http://www.loveisnotabuse.com/pdf/Liz%20Claiborne%20Relationship%20Abuse%20Hotsheet.pdf> (April 27, 2008).

5. Adapted from "Safety in Relationships: A Guide for Teens," *Children's Hospital Boston: Center for Young Women's Health, 1999–2008,* <http://www.youngwomenshealth.org/safety_in_relat.html> (April 27, 2008).

Chapter 8. Breaking Up and Starting Over

1. "Does Young Love Last?" *Scholastic Action*, September 4, 2000, p. 6.

2. Lev Grossman, "The Secret Love Lives of Teenage Boys," *Time,* September 4, 2006, pp. 40–41.

3. Dickinson, "Puppy Love's Bite," p. 82.

abstinence—Not having sex.

abuse—To treat with cruelty and violence.

adolescence—The period of time in which a young person develops from a child to an adult.

anxiety—A feeling of nervousness about future events.

body language—Gestures and movements that are a way of communicating without speaking.

clinical depression—A mental disorder in which feelings of sadness, hopelessness, and lack of interest in life persist for more than two weeks.

contraception—The intentional prevention of pregnancy.

crush—A brief but intense infatuation with someone.

curfew—The designated time a parent sets for a teen to be home.

depression—Feelings of sadness and hopelessness.

dopamine—A neurotransmitter associated with pleasurable sensations.

hormone—A chemical substance that signals the cells of the body to take some kind of action.

infatuation—An intense and brief passion for someone.

love—An intense feeling of caring for another person.

neurotransmitter—A chemical substance in the brain.

norepinephrine—A neurotransmitter associated with feelings of excitement.

peer pressure—Influence from one's peers, or people of the same age.

puberty—The stage of life when the body develops from that of a child to that of an adult.

serotonin—A brain chemical that affects emotions, including anxiety and depression.

STD—Sexually transmitted disease; an infection spread by sexual contact with an infected individual.

FURTHER READING

Fox, Annie, and Elizabeth Verdick. *The Teen Survival Guide to Dating & Relating: Real-World Advice on Guys, Girls, Growing Up, and Getting Along.* Minneapolis, Minn.: Free Spirit Publishing, 2005.

Packer, Alex J. *The How Rude! Handbook of Friendship & Dating Manners for Teens: Surviving the Social Scene.* Minneapolis, Minn.: Free Spirit Publishing, 2004.

Pfeifer, Kate Gruenwald. *American Medical Association Girl's Guide to Becoming a Teen.* San Francisco, Calif.: Jossey-Bass, The American Medical Association, 2006.

INTERNET ADDRESSES

Center for Young Women's Health
http://www.youngwomenshealth.org

National Teen Dating Abuse Helpline
http://www.loveisrespect.org

National Woman's Health Information Center: Girlshealth.gov
http://www.girlshealth.gov/relationships/

HOTLINE TELEPHONE NUMBERS

The National Domestic Violence Hotline
1-800-799-SAFE (7233)

The Youth Crisis Hotline
1-800-HIT-HOME (448-4663)

National Suicide Prevention Hotline
1-800-273-TALK (8255)

CONTRIBUTORS

Author **Dorothy Kavanaugh** is a freelance writer who lives near Philadelphia. She holds a bachelor's degree in elementary education from Bryn Mawr College. She has written many nonfiction titles for young adults.

Series advisor **Dr. Carroll Izard** is the Trustees Distinguished Professor of Psychology at the University of Delaware. His research and writing focuses on the development of emotion knowledge and emotion regulation and their contributions to social and emotional competence. He is author or editor of seventeen books (one of which won a national award) and more than one hundred articles in scientific journals. Dr. Izard is a fellow of both national psychological associations and the American Association for the Advancement of Science. He is the winner of the American Psychological Association's G. Stanley Hall Award and an international exchange fellowship from the National Academy of Sciences.

A Guys' Guide to Anger; A Girls' Guide to Anger
ISBN-13: 978-0-7660-2853-1   ISBN-10: 0-7660-2853-4

A Guys' Guide to Conflict; A Girls' Guide to Conflict
ISBN-13: 978-0-7660-2852-4   ISBN-10: 0-7660-2852-6

A Guys' Guide to Jealousy; A Girls' Guide to Jealousy
ISBN-13: 978-0-7660-2854-8   ISBN-10: 0-7660-2854-2

A Guys' Guide to Loneliness; A Girls' Guide to Loneliness
ISBN-13: 978-0-7660-2856-2   ISBN-10: 0-7660-2856-9

A Guys' Guide to Love; A Girls' Guide to Love
ISBN-13: 978-0-7660-2855-5   ISBN-10: 0-7660-2855-0

A Guys' Guide to Stress; A Girls' Guide to Stress
ISBN-13: 978-0-7660-2857-9   ISBN-10: 0-7660-2857-7

GUYS!

Nothing But
Girl Talk Ahead–
You've Been Warned!